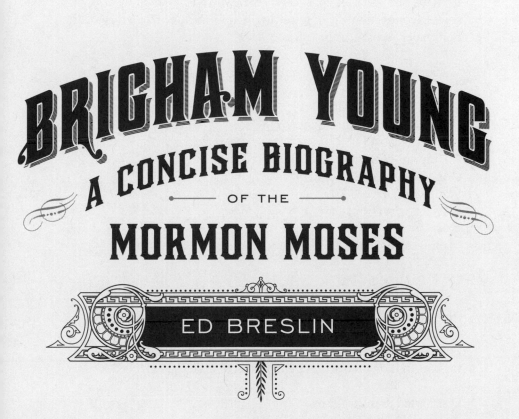

BRIGHAM YOUNG

A CONCISE BIOGRAPHY

OF THE

MORMON MOSES

ED BRESLIN

REGNERY
HISTORY

Cataloging-in-Publication data on file with the Library of Congress

ISBN 978-1-62157-040-0
Published in the United States by
Regnery History
An imprint of Regnery Publishing, Inc.
One Massachusetts Avenue NW
Washington, DC 20001
www.RegneryHistory.com

Manufactured in the United States of America

10 9 8 7 6 5 4 3 2 1

Books are available in quantity for promotional or premium use. Write to Director of Special Sales, Regnery Publishing, Inc., One Massachusetts Avenue NW, Washington, DC 20001, for information on discounts and terms, or call (202) 216-0600.

Distributed to the trade by
Perseus Distribution
250 West 57th Street
New York, NY 10107

THIS BOOK IS FOR

Eddie and June

Geoff and Janet

Gene and Cathy

CONTENTS

*"Preserve a steady, calm, and deliberate demeanor
and show that you are master of yourself."*
—BRIGHAM YOUNG, letter to his son John W. Young, July 31, 1873

•

*"I want my sons to realize and would be glad if all the world
could understand that no matter whether a man is a lawyer,
a doctor, a mechanic, or indeed, be he engaged
in any occupation whatever, that thorough honesty and integrity
will always lead to success, influence, and respect."*
—BRIGHAM YOUNG, letter to his son Alfales Young, September 21, 1875

•

*"I pray that the Spirit of Truth may find its way to each heart,
that we may all love the truth more than error, and cling
to that which is good that we may all be saved in
the kingdom of our God. Amen."*
—BRIGHAM YOUNG, sermon delivered on June 18, 1865

•

"Vengeance is mine and I have taken a little."
—BRIGHAM YOUNG, at the site of the makeshift monument
in Mountain Meadows, May 1861

CHAPTER 1

NEW ENGLAND
ROOTS

Brigham Young was a significant figure in the history of America and one of the great pioneers. Young, John C. Frémont, and Sam Houston make up the trinity of titans who built the American West. Yet, like Frémont, Brigham Young eventually overstepped the bounds of his power and tarnished his legacy.

Frémont fell from grace when, as a United States military officer, he attempted to retain the governorship of California despite orders from above to relinquish the position. He stood trial in Washington for his defiance and was convicted of mutiny and disobeying direct orders; years later, the impact of this public disgrace cost Frémont his chance at the presidency.

Brigham Young was guilty of more egregious acts of arrogance. He defied federal and local judiciary powers, dispensed vigilante justice, and practiced polygamy on a large scale. Finally, his seditious act of open rebellion against the president and the federal government forced the U.S. Army to take control of the Utah Territory. So Brigham Young, too, suffered irreparable damage to his image as a bold pioneer—as well as to the reputation he had built as a religious leader and a humanitarian. He was excoriated for these transgressions in his lifetime and has been condemned many times since. Yet despite the blemishes on his career, Brigham Young played a vital role in the settlement of the West. And his flaws had roots in the same soil as his achievements: his adopted religion, the Church of Jesus Christ of Latter-day Saints. Mormons were often at odds with those who considered their beliefs a deviation from orthodox Christianity and a threat to society's morals. What's more, the Latter-day Saints sought to govern their own communities without reference to duly elected or appointed federal, state, and local officials.

To this end the Latter-day Saints formed huge voting blocs and sought to influence or even control local and state politics. The result was resentment from non-Mormons and in many instances persecution of the Latter-day Saints. Hoping to gain enough political power to stop these persecutions, the church's founder, the prophet Joseph Smith, involved himself in politics to a still greater and more dangerous extent, eventually running for president of the United States. This overreach led to his murder by an outraged crowd in pioneering Carthage, Illinois, on June 27, 1844. To this day, Smith's followers consider him a martyr.

The murder of Joseph Smith was the galvanizing moment in the life of Brigham Young, one of Joseph Smith's closest colleagues and most ardent followers. After deft maneuvering, Young stepped into the leadership vacuum left by Smith's assassination and led the Saints with iron resolve for nearly three decades, during the time they established their church—and settled Utah—with remarkable energy and courage. From Utah, Mormonism, as their faith came to be called, spread throughout the United States and around the world. Today, global membership in the Church of Jesus Christ of Latter-day Saints numbers about fourteen million. Smith drew the plans; he was the architect. Young grew the organization; he was the builder.

⸺ • ⸺

Brigham Young was a quintessential American. His family had colonial roots in the harsh soil of New England. His father, John Young, born to Joseph Young and Betsey Hayden Treadway in 1763 in Hopkinton, Massachusetts, was one of six children. Brigham Young's grandfather Joseph was the son of a hardworking shoemaker named William Young, who had migrated south from New Hampshire to Hopkinton years earlier.

At the time Brigham's father John was born in 1763, his own father Joseph was a physician practicing in Hopkinton, a town surrounded by farms and about twenty-five miles outside Boston. Joseph also practiced medicine in nearby Framingham, shuttling back and forth between the two communities. The family was in good shape until Joseph was killed in an accident in 1769, when he was crushed beneath a felled tree.

The usual dreary scenario then ensued. First the family's farm and all their possessions were auctioned off to pay debts. Then town officials found new homes for the orphaned children as indentured laborers. John was bound over to a Colonel John Jones, a prosperous landowner. Life with the colonel was not pleasant; John had to endure frequent whippings from the colonel's harsh wife. In 1780, after ten years of this servitude, John joined the Continental Army at age sixteen. By the time the war ended three years later, John had served in three major campaigns under General George Washington. After the war John returned to Colonel Jones and hired out to him on a paying basis, no longer "bound over" for room and board only and no wages.

While working for Colonel Jones, John started to court Abigail Howe, three years his junior and one of five daughters of Phineas and Susanna Goddard Howe. The Howes lived nearby in Shrewsbury, Massachusetts, and were reasonably well off. Both Howe parents discouraged their daughter Abigail from spending time with John, a small and wiry orphan with extremely limited prospects.

Abigail, described as fair, blonde, and beautiful, ignored her parents and married John in 1785, two years after the end of the war. Her parents' misgivings about John Young proved prescient in this respect: life was hard for John and Abigail. It is likely that for the next sixteen years they were tenant farmers, eking out a livelihood from the unforgiving New England climate with its savage winters and its short growing season. By 1801, John and Abigail had eight children, and they decided to move west in search of a better life.

At that time there was a small land rush to the Deerfield Valley in southern Vermont, just a few miles north of the Massachusetts border. A dispute about the ownership of a large tract of land originally granted as a colonial patent had finally been settled. John managed to purchase fifty acres of this land for fifty dollars, a bargain even then. But the roads to southern Vermont were primitive in the extreme, just paths rutted by wagon wheels whenever the weather permitted wagons to traverse the land—only in summer or winter, when the mud was not prohibitively deep. Then again, in winter, snow could render the paths impassable except for sleds.

Undaunted, in January John loaded his family into one bobsled and his furniture and tools into another and started for the family's new home. The bobsleds were just crude boxes fashioned atop runners. John used horses to pull the sled transporting his family, but oxen pulled the sled loaded with the family's belongings. The hundred-mile trip in the dead of winter probably took ten days. The Berkshire Mountains in western Massachusetts and the Green Mountains in southern Vermont presented challenges. The family also had to contend with foul weather— sleet and icy rain, and maybe even a blizzard or two.

Yet they made it. In Whitingham they arranged to stay temporarily with an earlier settler and his family in the family's log cabin. Immediately John set to work to gather the tree trunks he would need to construct his own cabin, sixteen feet square. He found a clearing, dragged the poles into it, and, in the tradition of those settler times, constructed his cabin's walls in one day with the help of the neighboring men. That left only a few days of chinking the walls and adding the roof to finish the cabin.

In a matter of weeks the family settled into its own home. John and his sons immediately tapped the sugar maple trees. After boiling the sugar sap in a large kettle, they had pounds of maple sugar to barter for other necessities. This was a welcome development because the family had survived the winter and the arduous journey subsisting only on beef jerky, corn cakes, and small game, with an occasional deer thrown into the mix. Now they also had lots of maple syrup to spread on bread and cakes.

Spring was very welcome, and it came that first year in Vermont with an added bonus for the Young family. On the first day of June, Abigail gave birth to her ninth child and fourth son in the family's newly built cabin. She named him Brigham, her maternal grandparents' surname. Abigail must surely have been a stouthearted woman to have endured the tough winter passage while four months pregnant.

Yet her health would turn fragile. During the pregnancy she had suffered dizziness and the coughing fits that indicated "consumption"—a common affliction in those pre-antibiotic days; the deadly disease is now known as tuberculosis. The birthing left Abigail so weak that she could not attend to Brigham. Instead, he was bottle-fed by his older sister Fanny, thirteen at the time. Briggie, as the baby was called, clung to Fanny and accompanied her everywhere on her round of household and barnyard chores.

No one could know then that this healthy little baby boy was about to inaugurate a life with few equals, or that he would play an outsized part in the annals of the settlement of the American West. Before he died seventy-six years later, he would propagate a global religion, blaze a trail to the untamed West, colonize vast tracts of land, serve as first governor of the Utah Territory, establish the basis for the founding of Utah as a state, build Salt Lake City into the biggest town and key connection between St. Louis and San Francisco, found two world-class universities, and play an instrumental role in the completion of the transcontinental railroad, among countless other successful enterprises that led to his accumulation of a significant personal fortune. Brigham Young would do all this despite the handicap of only eleven days of formal education.

CHAPTER 2

BOYHOOD

— AND —

YOUTH

ife was hard for the Youngs. John Young's restlessness and deficiencies as a manager may have made it even harder. After Brigham's birth the family remained on their homestead in Whitingham for only three more years—three hard years that pitted the family against the stony and uncooperative soil of the Deerfield Valley. The Youngs had to do everything themselves: grow their food or hunt and trap it; spin, weave, and sew their clothing; tend to their livestock; churn their own butter; sugar off the maple trees; and make all of their meals. John and his sons also helped their neighbors and sometimes hired themselves out, usually for bartered supplies and necessities.

Pioneering for Americans truly began at Jamestown and at Plymouth Rock, though in those locations it did not yet involve prairie schooners and treks across the continent consuming many months. To put matters in perspective, 1804, when the Youngs abandoned southern Vermont,

Marble bust of
Brigham Young
in the Capitol Rotunda,
Washington, D.C.
U.S. Government Work

was the same year Lewis and Clark set out on their monumental journey of exploration. And only about a decade earlier, Daniel Boone had led a group of woodsmen that cleared and widened the path through the Cumberland Gap to enable wagons heading westward to use it. America was still in its infancy.

John Young, tired of the endless battle with the New England soil, led his family west into New York, having heard that the region offered fertile farmland. At Troy, New York, they ferried their two wagons across the wide Hudson River before continuing west along the Mohawk Valley until they reached the far side of the Alleghenies and Sherburne, a small settlement in Chenango County. A primitive pioneering settlement, Sherburne sat on a spit of land where the Chenango and the Susquehanna Rivers came together.

The new land did have good soil and plenty of game, both small and large, as well as edible plants and nuts. John and his sons set to work clearing land and building a log cabin after planting enough corn to see the family through the winter. Soon Abigail gave birth to a baby girl named Louisa. Three years later, in 1807, an eleventh and final child came along, a boy named Lorenzo Dow Young, named for America's first great itinerant preacher of the Bible. Though eccentric and unkempt, Dow was so famous at the time that Lorenzo became one of the most popular boys' names. Imagine this: Dow's autobiography outsold every book except the Bible. For the Young family, the joy of infant Lorenzo's arrival did not last long. Shortly afterward older sister Nabby died of tuberculosis at age eleven. There is little doubt that the young girl contracted this dreadful disease from her mother.

The same year daughter Nabby died, in late 1807, John moved his family to an area called "Dark Harbor," only a few miles from Sherburne. Again the family built and lived in a cabin. The Youngs continued to live in this greater Sherburne area for nine years, as Brigham went from a toddler to a teenager. During this period he grew tall and strong enough to work alongside his father and older brothers Joseph, four years his senior, and Phineas, two years older than Brigham. Father and sons would clear land and help build cabins and outbuildings for the settler families streaming into the area. Often they bartered this work for needed supplies. Brigham left graphic descriptions of how taxing this work could be, especially considering that in the central New York state winters, he rarely had proper clothing or enough to eat. This brutally hard existence inured Brigham at an early age to backbreaking work and to going without. Brigham later testified to the strictly economical ways of his father, and he would retain many of his father's lessons in economy and preserving resources throughout his life, even when he had become a very wealthy man.

During these early teen years, Brigham acquired the skills expected of a bright young man learning to make his livelihood on the frontier. Working alongside his father and his two older brothers, he learned to build sheds, barns, and even small houses. As a true country boy, he learned how to use a rifle and to hunt for game both large and small. He learned to fish in the region's abundant lakes, rivers, and streams. He also learned the techniques of a trapper and caught muskrat, otter, beaver, fox, mink, and other small game. From helping at the homestead, he learned how to plant and sow crops and how to harvest them. He also learned how to care for and handle livestock. Brigham Young remarked as an old man that he had had only eleven days of schooling—but he did receive a complete education in how to survive as a homesteading pioneer before he reached the age of twenty.

One event in 1809 would have a far-reaching effect on the family. That year, to great joy and considerable fanfare, Brigham's older sister Rhoda rejoined the family. She had stayed behind in Shrewsbury, Massachusetts, with her maternal Howe grandparents when the family moved to Whitingham, Vermont, in 1801. After an eight-year absence, Rhoda, now nineteen, joined the family in their cabin outside Sherburne. But she did not stay for long, leaving a scant four years later in 1839 when she married John P. Greene, a Methodist preacher. The newlyweds moved north to Aurelius, a town in Cayuga County, and settled a few miles above the northern tip of picturesque Cayuga Lake.

Restless as usual, and probably swayed by his son-in-law's glowing descriptions of Aurelius and its surroundings, John Young soon decided to follow Rhoda and her husband. Once again he moved his family, this time to Aurelius, within a short distance of his daughter Rhoda and John. It's more than likely that John Young hoped Rhoda, now twenty-three, would be able to lend a hand with raising her two youngest siblings— Louisa, nine, and Lorenzo Dow, six. Their mother probably had this same hope—her health continued to fail, and by this time her two eldest daughters had both married and moved away.

As it turned out, Rhoda's older sister Fanny left her husband, a womanizing alcoholic, and moved back in with her parents in their new home in Aurelius just in time to take care of her mother as her illness grew worse. Within two years of the move to Aurelius, Abigail lost her long, drawn-out battle with tuberculosis and died at age forty-nine in 1815. Even though she had long since been forced to surrender most of the duties of wife, mother, and homemaker, her death made a big hole in the fabric of the family. At a mere fourteen years of age, Brigham was far too young to lose his mother, to say nothing of Louisa and Lorenzo Dow, eleven and eight years old, respectively, when Nabby died.

For whatever reason, his wife's demise triggered another move for John Young. Taking his son Joseph, eighteen, his son Phineas, sixteen, and his fourteen-year-old son Brigham along with him, John migrated thirty-five miles farther west to a new homesteading site in Steuben County, near the town of Tyrone. Even though John and his sons had made the previous homestead in Aurelius quite comfortable, John did not hesitate to abandon it and head westward again to establish a new homestead at the tip of the wilderness.

John may well have been feeling overwhelmed by the loss of his wife, and he must have feared that he would prove inadequate at raising the two youngest children. As a result he left Louisa and Lorenzo Dow back in Aurelius with their older sister Rhoda and her preacher husband John. Rhoda and John were able to share the duties of parenting Louisa and Lorenzo Dow with another of Rhoda's older sisters, for by this time Susannah and her husband James Little had settled in the greater Aurelius area, near the town of Auburn. John's restlessness may well have been passed on to his daughter Rhoda, for she and her preacher husband John followed John Young west a few months later, in the fall of 1815. They brought along Lorenzo Dow, reuniting him with his father and his three older brothers. Louisa stayed behind in Aurelius with James and Susannah Little.

The Youngs were now living on the frontier. Only about a hundred miles from Lake Erie, Tyrone was not that far from present-day Ohio, which at the time was called simply the Western Reserve and considered the wilderness. Settlers were only then beginning to migrate that far west. John was able to purchase, on the cheap, one hundred acres, eighteen miles from the nearest settlement where he and the boys could buy supplies. In order to build a small cabin on their new land, John and his sons had to rely on themselves and on Daniel Kent, the husband of John's eldest daughter, Nancy. There were no neighbors to pitch in and help. Once again the new plot held sugar maple trees, and John and the boys set to "sugaring off" the sap and making sugar maple to sell or barter. As neighbors began to settle in the area, the Youngs again bartered their labor for needed supplies.

John Young seemed to have a tendency to do zany things, ill thought-out and non-nurturing, bordering on the irresponsible. While his older sons Joseph and Phineas were away working for other settlers, John left fourteen-year-old Brigham and eight-year-old Lorenzo Dow alone in the cabin while he traveled eighteen miles west to Painted Post, a trading establishment in what was still mostly Native American country. John wanted to trade his maple sugar for flour.

Back in the cabin, the two boys had nothing to eat. This was a condition Brigham had grown up with. He has left written evidence he often went hungry as a boy. Yet in this instance he showed the resourcefulness that would characterize his whole life, no matter the challenge. The boys spotted a stout robin in their yard. Possibly using the old single-shot musket his father had carried in the Revolutionary War, Brigham shot the robin, cleaned it back at the cabin, boiled it, and made it into a stew. By holding the empty flour barrel upside down and banging on it, the two boys managed to shake loose enough lodged flour to thicken the stew. Eating the stew and using up the last of the maple syrup their father hadn't taken along to barter at the trading post, the two boys managed to survive until John returned with a new supply of flour a day and a half later.

Such self-reliance would come in handy when two years later Brigham's life altered radically: from then on he would be called upon to care for himself on a permanent basis. In 1817, John Young returned from a trip back East with a new wife, the widow Hannah Brown. She arrived with several of her own children, and she would go on to have three more with John.

From the time of John Young's second marriage, he mostly separated from his former family. His daughter Susannah and her husband James Little took in Joseph and Lorenzo Dow, and Louisa was again living with her older sister Rhoda and Rhoda's preacher husband John Greene. For a short while Brigham also went back to Aurelius and lived with Susannah and James. When Brigham's father returned with new wife Hannah, he had told Brigham, all of sixteen years old, that he was on his own. Although Susannah's husband James was an enterprising Irishman, his and Susannah's financial circumstances were such that Brigham took his father's advice and sought paid employment.

He found a job in Auburn, the Cayuga county seat, not far from Aurelius. Bustling with a thousand residents, Auburn had a booming business district along its main street, Genesee Street, named for the nearby river. Shops and stores lined the entire length of the street. Brigham took a job in the woodworking shop of John C. Jeffries and began to learn the skills of a carpenter, painter, furniture maker, and glazier. The very first job Jeffries assigned him was to build a bedstead. Brigham did a solid job of it. During his entire youth and young manhood, Brigham learned fast and quietly. A quick study and a diligent worker, he took enormous pride in his skills and did every job, large or small, with assiduity and without complaint. He soon learned to make washboards, benches, chairs, and other more detailed and complicated household furniture.

During the next five years, Brigham stepped up his craftsmanship and became well known for building decorative mantelpieces to adorn the fireplaces of the houses that were being built in Auburn. He also constructed staircases and doorjambs and fittings, as well as louvered attic windows and other hallmarks of the Federalist architecture of this period. During this period, sometimes also called early Victorian, Federalist architecture was the transitional style between colonial or Georgian architecture and full and late Victorian architecture. The Federalist style flourished in America between the years 1780 and 1830. Many visitors to Auburn today are confidently told that Brigham Young made mantelpieces, staircases, and numerous pieces of furniture, especially desks and chairs. Brigham undoubtedly made many of these beautiful items, and experts who have examined them report that they represent excellent work.

Throughout these years Brigham was quiet, industrious, and fairly inconspicuous. Humble, he did not draw attention to himself. There were no early indications of the monumental leadership skills that would come to the fore a decade later. He did, however, demonstrate other skills. Having farmed with his father and his brothers, Brigham was able to cultivate the earth and raise crops to benefit himself and his family when still in his teens. Town lore also holds that he did some beautiful landscaping and gardening for homeowners, helping plan and plant gardens and orchards. Energetic in execution of his plans and fair in pricing his services, Brigham was in demand around town; his reliability and the quality of his work were givens.

At the age of twenty-one, Brigham was called upon to help his older sister Susannah when tragedy struck. She lost her industrious and clever husband James in an accident on his way home from town when his one-horse wagon overturned and crushed him. The law named Brigham one of his dead brother-in-law's executors. Another executor was Brigham's older brother Joseph. The documents settling this estate bear the earliest known signatures by Brigham Young.

A year later, in early 1823, Brigham moved from Auburn eight miles north to Bucksville because of better opportunities along the banks of the Erie Canal. The first boat to traverse the canal had arrived at Bucksville only three years earlier, on the morning of May 31, 1820. Brigham went to Bucksville looking to participate in the boom the canal had set off. He quickly found odd jobs repairing furniture and houses and constructing and painting canal boats. Before long the quality of his work induced Charles Parks to hire Brigham full time. Parks owned a business producing furniture, pails, and buckets. Parks gave Brigham a great deal of responsibility and paid him $2.50 a week.

Local lore holds that Brigham invented a clever pigment crusher for mixing paints. Using a cannonball his father had brought home from the Revolutionary War as a pestle, Brigham pounded pigments in a big iron pot that served as the mortar. The new method used a supply of water to facilitate the mixing of oil and lead with the crushed pigment. During this time Brigham is also reported to have stopped a mill wheel and dived into the water to retrieve from the bottom a small child who had fallen in. He might have saved the child's life had the panicked mother not wrenched the child from him as he performed artificial respiration. Yet another tale relates how Brigham saved the Parks factory when lightning struck and sparks ignited the wood shavings. He organized a bucket brigade and nipped the fire in time, before it flared out of control. This is one of the earliest instances of Brigham Young's on-the-spot resourcefulness as an organizer and leader.

The first reports of Brigham as a public speaker also come from this time in Bucksville. He helped set up the Bucksville Forensic and

Oratorical Society and was an avid participant in debates and other public speaking contests. Researching subjects for the debates may well have served to supplement Brigham's scanty formal education. And he is alleged to have spoken so humorously once about a type of over-confident, know-it-all young man that the laughter got to a certain young man in the audience, who assumed that Brigham was making fun of him. The young man challenged Brigham to a fistfight. Protesting that he was not a fighting man, Brigham nevertheless proclaimed that he was prepared to defend himself and would let the chips fall where they might as to who ended up taking a beating. The offended challenger backed off. Brigham was a popular and formidable young man. His charisma and determination would one day play on a much larger stage than Bucksville.

CHAPTER 3

FAMILY MAN

Brigham's boss Charles Parks had a great friend who lived near the workshop. His name was Asa Works and he, like Brigham's father John Young, had fought in the Revolutionary War. Asa and his wife Abigail had a beautiful eighteen-year-old daughter named Miriam Evangeline Works, blonde, blue-eyed, and possessed of a winning personality and a placid disposition. The Works family had migrated west from Massachusetts to central New York, just like the Youngs. Originally they had lived in Worcester, Massachusetts. That was not far from Hopkinton, where Brigham's father John had lived until the untimely death of Brigham's physician grandfather ruined the family's fortunes and rendered John and his siblings scattered orphans.

Brigham was introduced to Miriam and began to spend time with her. There was a strong mutual attraction, and in no time Brigham was openly courting her. They married in early October 1824. Gilbert Weed, the justice of the peace in Aurelius, performed the ceremony at a tavern owned by James Pine and located between Auburn and Bucksville. For a few months, the newlyweds lived in a rented log cabin on a farm owned by friends, right near the Parks factory. But Brigham set to work quickly building a new home and completed it before the year was out. This house in Aurelius was a kind of modified Cape Cod, about 400 square feet, typical for the time. It had a fireplace and two bedrooms, a living room, a dining room, a modest kitchen, and a small front porch. Brigham and Miriam joined the Methodist church and settled into community life. Eleven months after they married, on September 26, 1825, Miriam gave birth to their first child, a little girl named Elizabeth.

That same year Bucksville was renamed Port Byron, most likely in honor of Lord Byron, the celebrated English poet. Brigham and his young family lived there without incident and in apparent happiness for the next three years, until Brigham took a job with a contractor building a tannery forty miles north on the shores of Lake Ontario in the town of Oswego. The family briefly moved to Oswego and the tannery went up fast. By the end of 1828, Brigham was on the move again, taking his family to join his father and many of his brothers and sisters, who were now clustering around the town of Mendon, about fifty miles southwest of Oswego, near the bustling port city of Rochester. John Young had moved to Mendon a year earlier, after selling the homestead in Tyrone. For a short while, Brigham, Miriam, and Elizabeth lived with his father and stepmother Hannah. Then Brigham broke ground and built a house and workshop on a piece of his father's land.

The Young clan was sticking together once again. Soon Brigham's widowed sister Susannah Little, her daughter Louisa, and Louisa's husband Joel Sanford lived in Mendon, as well as Rhoda and her husband John Greene. Phineas and John Jr. lived in nearby towns. Joseph lived with his father and stepmother Hannah as did, occasionally for long stretches, Brigham's youngest brother, Lorenzo Dow. Brigham's sister

Fanny, who had left her husband years earlier, also lived in Mendon with the family of Heber Chase Kimball. Kimball, from this point on a lifelong friend to Brigham, has left testimony that the Youngs were not prosperous, suffered much sickness and hardship, and were not accepted in the upper social circles of Mendon society. They were not embraced by the established church in Mendon and instead became Methodists.

Brigham gained a second daughter when Miriam gave birth to Vilate on June 1, 1830, Brigham's twenty-ninth birthday. Miriam named her new daughter for her best friend, Vilate Kimball, Heber's wife. Then, for about the next year and a half, Brigham moved his family to a small rented house near Canandaigua while he hired out to help a prosperous local farmer build a substantial new house. When the house was finished, Brigham and his family moved back to Mendon.

But tragedy struck when Miriam came down with tuberculosis and was rendered a semi-invalid. This disease had afflicted Brigham's mother and taken her life at age forty-nine, and now his wife was similarly afflicted. The family suffered. Because Miriam could not take care of herself and their two daughters, Brigham had to cut his work hours and do mostly part-time jobs. He had to carry Miriam from bed to a rocking chair by the fireplace each morning and back to bed each evening. In between he had to prepare the meals and see to the care and feeding of the children. He could steal hours away for handyman work, but he could not sustain a full-time job or tackle a large project. So caring and nurturing was Brigham that the local newspaper carried a letter attesting to his fine Christian character as both husband and father. As he had been viewed everywhere, so too at Canandaigua and Mendon, Brigham was held in high regard by neighbors and townsfolk.

Today, Mendon is a prosperous suburb of Rochester. Both there and in the greater Rochester area, evidence abounds of Brigham's presence in the four years he lived there in the late 1820s and the early 1830s. His workshop in Mendon was well-known and busy. Having been on his own for eleven years by the time he set it up, he had mastered many skills. At the University of Rochester and in small museums in Mendon and in nearby communities, there are papers on exhibit signed by Brigham, many of them promissory notes having to do with business. Numerous pieces of furniture Brigham made are also on display, some bearing a distinct letter "B" he stamped on his work. He also put this "B" on crockery and on bricks he fired in a kiln in his shop. One exhibit shows a lathe on which Brigham is believed to have turned out legs for chairs and other pieces of furniture.

The site of the shop itself has been excavated, and ample evidence has been found that Brigham's range of skills by this time was breathtaking by today's standards. Not only had he mastered carpentry, but he also appears to have been skilled as a blacksmith and metalworker as well. He most likely shod his own horses and mules. Apparently, he was also adept at making hand-tooled nails, locks, keys, iron hinges, and spikes. Excavation at the site uncovered a vast collection of metalworking and woodworking tools, as well as farming and gardening tools and implements, all of which Brigham would have used.

At the site of Brigham's nearby house, there is ample evidence that he tilled and worked the land. Seeds have been uncovered from many forms of fruits, berries, and crops. He was applying the lessons in agriculture he had learned when helping his father. The land around Mendon—in fact the land south of Rochester in general—has rich soil, ideal for farming. It was much better land than the Youngs had known at any of their previous homesteads, going all the way back to Massachusetts. Besides the farming and gardening opportunities offered by the rich loam in this area, the game both small and large was plentiful, and the fishing in the many rivers and streams was excellent.

Compared to the harsh scarcity, hunger, and deprivation Brigham and the rest of the Young family had known up until this time, Mendon and vicinity must have seemed like an earthly paradise, a land of milk and honey. Despite the hardship of caring for his invalided wife Miriam and shouldering all the parenting responsibilities for their two daughters, Brigham must have felt blessed during the years the family lived here. Among other items found in the archaeological digs at Brigham's home and shop, handmade toys surfaced as well, probably fashioned by Brigham for his daughters. At this time in his life, he seems to have been an ideal husband and father.

Brigham's friend Heber Kimball wrote about how industrious both he and Brigham were as young men during these years in Mendon. Without hesitation the two hired out to farmers in summer and fall. When the crops had to be harvested, they worked in the fields from sunup to sundown. During these spells of hiring out, Brigham relied on help from his family; his parents and his siblings pitched in to care for his young daughters. Kimball wrote descriptions of working alongside Brigham in winter, chopping wood in snow waist-high to earn eighteen cents per cord cut. The two would often work long hours in exchange for fifty cents a day, or sometimes for a small prearranged barter in crops or supplies.

Presumably by the time Brigham had his shop going full blast, such rigorous days as a hired-out laborer were behind him. He had built a large undershot waterwheel that powered his shop. Even though he had almost no formal schooling, by his late twenties he was an accomplished farmer, landscaper, gardener, brick-maker, painter, glazier, carpenter, cabinetmaker, metalworker, boatwright, and blacksmith.

Over the whole course of Brigham's life, his practicality, thriftiness, and industry show through—all learned from parents John and Abigail Young. His parents had also grounded their children in the basic tenets of Christianity, and the Bible was in frequent use in the Young household all the while Brigham lived there. As a testament to the strong religious atmosphere in the Young household, recall that John and Abigail named their youngest son for the great itinerant preacher Lorenzo Dow, who for years was loosely affiliated with the Methodist Church, the dominant religion in the Young household. Brigham's practical skills, combined with the staunch religious principles of his traditional Methodist upbringing, helped him earn high marks as a man of honor, dignity, and substance in every community he had lived in.

But Brigham was about to undergo a religious transformation that would lead him to a destiny he had no inkling of yet. His life was about to change irrevocably.

CHAPTER 4

CONVERSION

Conversion to the Church of Latter-day Saints came to Brigham indirectly and gradually. There was no dramatic Saul-on-the-road-to-Damascus moment. When Brigham was growing up, his family had been immersed in the study of the Bible. The Youngs had affiliated themselves with the Methodist Church, and some of Brigham's brothers had even become preachers for that denomination. The Methodists were very strong at this time in America and especially successful in their efforts to gain converts among the frontier communities. This was the time of the Second Great Awakening in America, the First having come in the early decades of the eighteenth century in colonial times. The Second Awakening began in 1790, when the new republic was in its infancy, and lasted for about fifty years, to 1840. During this period central and western New York State came to be known as the "Burned Over District" because of the frequency of fiery sermons and emotionally heated camp revival meetings staged there by mostly Methodist and Baptist preachers looking for converts. Some of these meetings would become so supercharged with emotion that people would speak in tongues, and incidents of holy rolling occurred as well.

These American camp revival meetings owed a debt of origin to the revivalists' "Holy Fairs" held in Scotland in the early years of the eighteenth century, promoted by the Presbyterian Church. A camp meeting could last for days or a few weeks or even as long as a month. Both itinerant preachers and local preachers from miles around would travel to the camp site and preach for hours in a nonstop relay designed to impress on the listeners the vital importance of embracing, in a personal act of faith, God and his Bible, and especially the Gospels. Just as the new republic had proclaimed all men equal politically, so the Second Awakening proclaimed all men equal religiously, in the sight of God. All were therefore free to establish a direct link to God.

The Methodists and the Baptists were the two most active denominations proselytizing this new, American approach to religion. Many Americans had been confused by the different choices available among the Protestant denominations imported from Europe. These older European forms of Christianity tended to be more structured and more hierarchical, with priests or other members of the hierarchy acting as spokesman and intermediaries between God and the ordinary people. Methodists and Baptists simplified and personalized the approach to God and declared that a direct relationship with God, without benefit of clergy or of any form of church hierarchy, was possible to all people, no matter how humble their origins, scanty their education, or scarce their possessions.

Religious fervor centered on the Bible was in the air all during Brigham Young's childhood, youth, and early manhood. Numerous reports exist that when Brigham was a practicing Methodist he was a good Christian in faith, thought, and deed. As we have seen, he was respected and admired in every community he had lived and worked in. There was no question that God was important to Brigham and that he believed the Bible was the good book—especially the Gospels that retold the life of Jesus Christ. The same was true for Brigham's next older brother, Phineas, two years Brigham's senior. Phineas had become an itinerant Methodist preacher, called a "circuit rider," before settling down in Victor, a small town very near Mendon, where he served as the highly respected resident preacher at the local Methodist church.

Then one fateful day in early April 1832, Phineas dropped into the Tomlinson Inn near Mendon and met a young preacher having his lunch. The young preacher was named Samuel Smith, and he carried with him a book written by his brother Joseph—purporting to be a new sacred scripture containing a new divine revelation. Titled *The Book of Mormon*, the new scripture explained the Bible in a new way and also gave a history of Christianity in the New World before Europeans arrived. In the book, Samuel's brother Joseph explained that the new revelation had been delivered in a vision, when the angel Moroni appeared to him in a field. The angel directed Joseph to a site where golden plates that told these ancient truths were buried. Joseph went and uncovered them, translated them into English, and, through the largesse of an early convert who believed in Joseph wholeheartedly, published them as *The Book of Mormon*. The book, printed in Palmyra, fifteen miles from Mendon, was stirring excitement and controversy in the area.

Phineas purchased a copy of the book, thinking that he would debunk it. As a practicing Methodist minister, Phineas felt confident he could expose the book's errors and prove it a fraud. That was his purpose as he took the book home. Samuel Smith had told Phineas that he knew the book to be a revelation and a gift from the Holy Ghost, and that he had no doubt that his brother Joseph was a prophet and a seer. Phineas had his doubts. But these disappeared after Phineas studied the new book thoroughly for a week. Finding no errors, Phineas came to believe the book was valid in all its aspects. So thinking, he gave it to his father John to read. Once John Young read it, he became more enthusiastic than Phineas. Next Phineas took the book to his sister Fanny, who had married so poorly and was now separated from her ne'er-do-well husband. Fanny read the book closely and embraced it as a stunning revelation.

Fanny in turn urged Brigham to read the book. Sober and skeptical, Brigham read *The Book of Mormon* thoroughly and took his time in analyzing it. He strove to assure himself that its revelations were valid and that they accorded with and furthered the understanding of traditional scripture. Brigham also wanted to reserve judgment until he had time to appraise the people behind this remarkable book. He needed to know that they were solid people of probity and character and not sensationalizing opportunists. The truth was that the whole area around Mendon had been alive with rumors about the "Gold Bible" since it came off the presses in March of 1830. Certainly the Youngs had heard all about it; Brigham must have been aware of it long before Phineas purchased that fateful copy from Samuel Smith.

A friend of Phineas named Solomon Chamberlain proved instrumental in the Youngs' accepting the new book of scripture. A recent convert to Mormonism, Solomon too had previously been an itinerant Methodist preacher. When Phineas, out riding the circuit and preaching, stayed overnight with Solomon, he listened as Solomon explained the heavenly authority vested in *The Book of Mormon*. The book was the product of direct intervention from heavenly sources, Solomon explained. Then he added that to act as a messenger for God, one had to have received authorization from a direct heavenly source. This had not occurred for eighteen centuries before the angel Moroni appeared in a vision to Joseph Smith. Because of this direct connection to the

divine, Joseph Smith and those he ordained as elders had a priestly sanction placed upon them that no other Protestant sect or denomination
had. Only the Catholic Church had claimed such a direct heavenly connection established by divine authority, and all Protestant sects and
denominations had declared the Catholic Church to be apostate and
therefore invalid.

This meant that the new religion established by Joseph Smith was
the only one now extant with a valid charter from heaven to be guided
by ministers ordained as priests and called elders. Like almost all the
Youngs, Phineas had long been searching for the one true and valid path
to salvation and immortality. After listening to Solomon Chamberlain
expound on the divine source and impregnable validity of *The Book of
Mormon*, Phineas ceased to act as a Methodist preacher and drifted in
thoughtful perplexity for a short while. As a messenger of God espous-
ing the Methodist faith Phineas now considered himself, in the light of
what Solomon Chamberlain explained to him, no longer sanctioned to
preach.

A short while later Phineas, despite his doubts, attended a Reformed
Methodist Church conference at Oswego, where Solomon Chamberlain
proposed *The Book of Mormon* as a divine instance of scriptural revelation. In a voice vote, the attendees rejected the book and Solomon
Chamberlain as well. At that instant Phineas felt compelled to stand up
and defend the book and his friend.

While at this point Phineas had clearly embraced the new book and
its divine revelations, Brigham and several members of the Young family
still drifted in confusion and doubt, with reservations holding them back.
The Book of Mormon was flat-out controversial. Then an event occurred
that dispelled all doubts and reservations for Phineas, Brigham, and
Brigham's friend Heber Chase Kimball. In the autumn of 1831, five Mormon elders from Columbia, Pennsylvania, traveled to the Mendon area
as missionaries and proceeded to preach. Though not highly educated or

particularly eloquent, these five emissaries spoke from the heart so plainly, so convincingly, and so forcefully that the people of Mendon were greatly moved. Brigham Young and his best friend Heber Chase Kimball heard these five elders preach to life-changing effect. Kimball later wrote a description of the dramatic impact the testimony of these missionaries had on him and his friend Brigham, and how convinced they both were of the truth and efficacy of the new religion by the passion, intensity, and devoutness these men embodied.

Years later, in the original temple in Salt Lake City, Brigham Young spoke of the power and glory these five elders from Pennsylvania projected so eloquently yet plainly. Brigham said that after he heard them he was certain that Joseph Smith was a prophet touched by divine intervention and that the Holy Ghost had inspired Joseph Smith to translate the golden tablets revealed by the angel Moroni. After hearing the Pennsylvania elders bear witness, Brigham stood convinced that *The Book of Mormon* was the key to the heavenly salvation and immortality he had been searching for all his life.

Yet Brigham was too steady and stable to act on an impulse. That's why in the late fall he and his brother Phineas and Heber Kimball undertook a strenuous trek to Columbia, Pennsylvania, to consult further with the five elders who had visited them a few months earlier. Such a journey of over a hundred and twenty miles through snow and ice and over mountains with frozen creeks and streams was extremely difficult in those postcolonial days of primitive roads and paths. Yet the three men reached Columbia safely and spent several days there visiting with the five elders, asking questions, and listening to the answers. They also attended services and heard the elders preach again.

With their questions answered and their knowledge of the new religion and of *The Book of Mormon* greatly expanded, Brigham, Phineas, and Heber returned to Mendon. Brigham, not yet a baptized convert to the new religion but enveloped in his new fervor, sought a consultation with his highly respected older brother Joseph, who, at the time, was preaching in Canada as a Methodist circuit rider. After listening to Brigham, Joseph was convinced that his younger brothers had found the religion the family had been seeking for over a quarter of a century. Joseph therefore returned to Mendon with Brigham.

The Youngs undertook large and important decisions as a family. With the patriarch John and his sons Joseph, Phineas, and Brigham all convinced of the glory and efficacy of *The Book of Mormon* and the new religion founded by Joseph Smith, the Youngs took further action. Guided by Phineas, John and Joseph traveled back to Columbia, Pennsylvania, in the early spring for further consultation and instruction from the five elders and their congregation. The Youngs were now total believers, and on April 5, 1832, John and Phineas were baptized as Saints. The following day Joseph followed suit. Brigham would have joined them in Pennsylvania but for his domestic obligations back home in Mendon, with his wife so ill from tuberculosis.

That explains why one of the five elders from the Columbia branch, Eleazer Miller, accompanied the Youngs on their trek back to Mendon. When they reached Mendon, they found Brigham waiting for them in great anticipation. He had been caring for his ill wife Miriam and his two young daughters, but his mind had been on his desire to join the new religion. Thus Eleazer Miller lost no time in performing the most significant baptismal ceremony of his life, converting Brigham and confirming him as a member of the Church of Christ of Latter-day Saints on the momentous date of April 14, 1832. In later years, Brigham would refer to this day as his "re-birthday." It was a snowy day and the baptism was performed at the water's edge in a nearby river, two miles from Brigham's house and shop. When the party of men returned to Brigham's house, Eleazer Miller, obviously recognizing greatness in Brigham, placed his hands upon the new convert and pronounced him an elder.

In the end, Brigham had become convinced that the Saints—especially Joseph Smith and his brother Samuel—were sincere and inspired people, and he embraced the new religion with all his heart and soul. In that spring of 1832, almost all of Brigham's immediate family converted to Mormonism and were baptized in it. By October of the following year, most of Brigham's extended family had also been converted and baptized as Latter-day Saints. This apparently simple chain of events set off an otherworldly transformation in Brigham Young, a conversion that galvanized him and ultimately led him to become a key figure in the settlement of the American West—the Mormon Moses, who led the Latter-day Saints from persecution to their promised land flowing with milk and honey.

CHAPTER 5

MISSIONARY

Brigham Young never did anything by half measures. And he would need all the strength his newfound faith imparted to face the challenges that soon confronted him. His beloved wife Miriam was failing more every day, growing weaker with every strained breath, as she fought against the onslaught of consumption, the same disease that had deprived Brigham of his adored mother when he was barely more than a boy. Today most forms of tuberculosis are treatable with antibiotics, but back then in pioneer days, it was a death sentence. When someone so afflicted coughed up blood, it was—as in the famous case of John Keats, the great English poet and another victim of the disease—a clear sign that that person's days on earth were numbered. Despite the despondency his wife's failing health caused Brigham, he nevertheless shared with her his joy at conversion to the Saints. Hearing this, Miriam struggled to keep her disease at bay long enough to be schooled in the new religion by her husband. Brigham preached and explained *The Book of Mormon* to her, and when the weather broke and became sufficiently warm for Miriam to be transported the two miles to the river, Brigham rejoiced in her baptism.

Then Brigham and Heber Chase Kimball wasted no time in getting out the word. Heber Chase Kimball's wife Vilate had been caring for her best friend Miriam and her two daughters, Elizabeth, seven, and Vilate, two, ever since Brigham and Heber had traveled that winter to Columbia to consult with the Pennsylvania elders. And after Brigham and Heber returned to Mendon, Miriam stayed on in the Kimball house with her two daughters while Brigham and Heber traveled as missionaries to preach their newfound religion to others in their region. Their enthusiasm for missionary work was indicative of the fervor each had for their new faith, and is an early indication of why both men would later be named among the Twelve Apostles, when the best of the elders were chosen to guide the new religion. But all that was years in the future. The two missionaries spent the summer of 1832 traveling to towns in western New York. In *Brigham Young: American Moses*, biographer Leonard J. Arrington reports that Brigham and Heber visited the western New York towns of Hector, Henrietta, Reading, Hornby, Patten, Avon, and Warsaw. It's likely that in their enthusiasm the two visited many other towns and hamlets in western and central New York State as well.

After placing his dying wife and his two daughters in the care of Vilate Kimball, Brigham significantly proceeded to divest himself of all earthly goods and possessions, simply abandoning them where they stood. His shop and house, it seems, were never used again. Brigham wrote later that he had no fear when doing this because he knew that his faith would see to it that his needs were provided for. He placed his confidence in the Saints and in their strong and unshakeable relationship with God.

Earlier in the spring, shortly after his baptism, Brigham had visited the Kimball house only to walk in on the beginning of a prayer circle. One of the five great elders from Columbia, Pennsylvania, was visiting Mendon to preach at the time. His name was Alpheus Gifford, and he had been highly instrumental in converting the Youngs and the Kimballs. After kneeling down in the available space, which meant kneeling so that his back was to the others because they were so squeezed for space, Brigham began to speak in tongues at the very same moment as Gifford, facing in the opposite direction, did the same thing. The two men spoke in tongues in perfect harmony and everyone present was amazed, including Gifford and Brigham themselves—what had happened was miraculous. This instance of divine inspiration only fired Brigham's resolve to preach the word even more, no matter how far he had to range. He later wrote how he felt empowered by God to preach despite his limited education because the Spirit had so invested and lifted him. Brigham felt that God was in control, working through him and guiding him when he preached. He was convinced that his preaching was guided by divine power, just as he was convinced that as long as he lived in obedience and harmony with Divine Will all his earthly needs would be taken care of.

After spending the summer preaching on the road with Heber, Brigham returned home, only to find tragedy would again visit him there. On September 8, 1832, his wife Miriam died, praising the Lord with her final breath. She died of consumption as had Brigham's mother—Miriam's lungs having filled with fluid and given out. Once again, Brigham was bereft of the woman he most cherished and loved on the face of the earth. It cannot have been easy for him. He had lost his adored mother when scarcely into his teen years, and now, as a robust young man in his thirty-first year, he lost his adored wife Miriam after only eight short years of marriage. He and Miriam had lived just one short summer together with daughters Elizabeth and Vilate as a family of Latter-day Saints.

The premature losses of the two women he most loved traumatized Brigham at some deep level, yet his character carried him through these wrenching and potentially debilitating losses. With this latest loss of Miriam, he also had the strength and comfort provided by his new religion, fortified by the compassion and all-encompassing love found among the community of Saints. They rallied to help him bear his grief. And Brigham did not falter or repine. He grieved deeply but immediately resolved to pursue his calling as an elder—to seek more converts. In order to be properly equipped for this mission, he felt compelled to meet Joseph Smith Jr., the prophet, and to see the central community the Saints had established in Kirtland, Ohio, a few miles east of Cleveland.

Kirtland was important. Joseph Smith Jr. emphasized to his followers the importance of "gathering" and forming a tight-knit community. In Kirtland he established a template for communities the Saints would establish throughout their history. Their migrations would be undertaken always with the intent of fulfilling Smith's prophecy that America was Zion: Smith taught that the dispersed ten tribes of Israel would be reunited, "gathered" in America, and thereby achieve fulfillment of the biblical promise. In Kirtland the Saints built their first temple and founded their first community. Joseph Smith Jr. had traveled there in January of 1831, and by the time Brigham undertook his journey to Kirtland with his brother Joseph and his best friend Heber Chase Kimball in the autumn of 1832, the community was rapidly building and expanding as the first headquarters of the Latter-day Saints.

As the three pilgrims worked their way west to Kirtland, they stopped along the way at various homes in newly founded communities of Saints. They carried letters of introduction with them and, while staying with the families of Saints who welcomed them, they attended services and prayer circles and, as elders, discussed and preached the new teachings

The Latter-day Saints Temple in Kirtland, Ohio. *Library of Congress*

laid out in *The Book of Mormon*. When Brigham, Joseph, and Heber reached Kirtland, they had ready accommodations because their sister Rhoda and her husband John P. Greene had already resettled there from Mendon. Immediately upon arrival the three set out to find Joseph Smith Jr., but when they called at his house they learned that he was out working in the fields. Directed there, they finally came upon him as he wielded an ax in working clothes, covered with sweat and shavings from chopping wood.

Brigham was impressed and awed with Smith. The two young men took to each other immediately. Brigham later wrote about how over-whelmed he was to shake the hand of a man who had undergone a divine intervention and received the teachings inscribed on the sacred golden tablets revealed to him by the angel Moroni. And it did not take long for Smith to be impressed by Brigham's intelligence, intensity, and devoutness. As was the custom among Saints, Smith invited the three pilgrims to return to his house and take supper there. Joseph's wife Emma had long since grown accustomed to her husband's inviting newly arrived believers to their home to share an impromptu meal and conversation.

As would be expected, the mealtime discussion revolved around theological and spiritual matters, and before long Brigham was moved to speak in tongues. Most of those present had never heard someone speak in tongues before, and they were naturally taken aback—and some were downright skeptical. After the meal, out of earshot of Brigham, these skeptics asked Smith what he thought of such a phenomenon. Expecting Smith to dismiss Brigham's inspired act as unorthodox and invalid, these doubters were surprised to hear Smith explain that, guided by God, Brigham had spoken in the ancient Adamic language. Smith was renowned for his acute sensitivity and his ability to see people whole even upon first introduction, and he startled his dinner guests that night by predicting that Brigham would someday lead their church—a prediction that would turn out to be accurate.

The trip to Kirtland had a profound effect upon the Young brothers. After they returned to Mendon, Brigham and Joseph lingered only a short while before undergoing the vicissitudes of a winter trek north into Canada to convert the former congregants of Joseph's Methodist circuit riding days to the new religion. The previous winter, Brigham had made this same arduous journey to consult with Joseph and to bring him the teachings of *The Book of Mormon* after visiting in Pennsylvania with the five elders of Columbia. Now the two brothers set out together on this 250-mile winter trek to reach the frontier communities formerly ministered to by circuit-riding Joseph as a Reformed Methodist minister.

Having both formerly been members of the Reformed Methodist Church, Joseph and Brigham knew exactly how to approach and explain to the Canadian settlers the new teachings and remarkable revelations of *The Book of Mormon*. The two brothers spent six weeks travelling to various scattered settlements in what was then called "Upper Canada." Their trip was successful, they baptized many converts, and in their wake they left the beginnings of the first Canadian communities of Saints. This marked the first successful international mission of a church that would become famous for its missionary work on a global scale. When Brigham and Joseph returned home in February, they crossed the border into New York from Kingston, Ontario, by walking across Lake Ontario on the ice. Once back home in Mendon, they continued to preach and proselytize in the towns of western New York State. In between times, having shed his earthly possessions, Brigham hired out as a workman, drawing upon the many skills he had acquired as a carpenter, farmer, glazier, builder, painter, and all-around handyman. All this time his daughters were safely cared for by the Kimballs, with whom they lived and with whom Brigham stayed when in Mendon.

A few months later, when the weather broke in the spring, Brigham set out again for Upper Canada. He sought to make more converts and to visit the new communities of Saints he and his brother Joseph had established a few months earlier, back in the winter. The first place Brigham visited was the town of Lyons, where he had found Joseph preaching as a Reformed Methodist a year and a half earlier when he needed to consult with him about *The Book of Mormon*. Brigham baptized converts in Lyons and left a small new branch of Saints in his wake. A new convert there, Jonathon Hampden, was so inspired and enthusiastic that Brigham ordained him as an elder and the two traveled together back across the New York border to Indian River Falls, where they made several more converts. Among these converts were David W. Patten, who would later join Brigham and Heber as one of the original Twelve Apostles, and Warren Parrish, so able that he would eventually serve as one of Joseph Smith's personal secretaries.

Brigham and Jonathon crossed the border yet again and checked on the small community near West Laboro established that past winter by Brigham and Joseph. When three families there expressed an interest in joining the main community in Kirtland, Brigham guided them there in July before returning to Mendon. No sooner had Brigham arrived back in Mendon than he found himself packing up with the Kimballs and his two daughters for their own migration in late September to Kirtland, to take up permanent residence in the growing community of Saints. By the time Brigham got to Kirtland, he had traveled over two thousand miles in a little over a year's time, preaching and spreading the word for the new faith as embodied in *The Book of Mormon*. Astonishingly, he had done most of his traveling on foot, only occasionally hitching rides in crude wagons or traveling by boat. He had become a prophet afire, preaching out of ironclad conviction a new faith based on divine revelation.

CHAPTER 6

KIRTLAND

W hen Brigham arrived in Kirtland in the fall of 1833, the town
had been "gathering" Saints for nearly two years. There was a
building boom in full swing as new converts poured in from
New England, New York, and Pennsylvania at a steady rate of several
hundred a year. So many new Saints crowded into the rapidly expanding
town that there was more manpower than there was work. In order to
support themselves and their families, many of the new arrivals started
to branch out into the surrounding countryside to hire out their skills
or labor in exchange for cash or barter.

This situation briefly presented a dilemma for Brigham. He needed
a way to provide for himself and his two young daughters, yet he wanted
to stay right in Kirtland to be near Joseph Smith at all times. Brigham
and his daughters stayed with his sister Rhoda and her husband John
Greene, so they had a temporary home right from the start, and soon

thereafter Heber Kimball rented a small house where his family and Brigham and his two daughters were able to live as they had back in Mendon. But Brigham still faced the task of finding a way to support himself and his two daughters without leaving Kirtland. As he had when he abandoned all his possessions and made the trip to Kirtland the previous year—even arriving there in borrowed clothes—Brigham again placed his trust in God and in the community of Saints to provide.

He was not disappointed. He set to work hiring out for cash or barter and before long was involved in building homes. He engaged to build a house for a Saint named Andrew Cahoon though at the time the deal was made Cahoon was uncertain he would be able to compensate Brigham for his services. As it turned out, Cahoon obtained the money and was able to pay Brigham by the time the house was complete. Brigham took this as a good sign. He also built a house in Kirtland for his friends Heber and Vilate Kimball and constructed a third for John Smith, an uncle of Joseph Smith. In pursuing this almost spiritual approach to providing for his family, Brigham learned a valuable lesson in proceeding in good faith and leaving the rest up to God. He learned to take the appropriate step within his control at the moment and to trust in divine providence that good results, out of his control, would nevertheless materialize through grace.

One seemingly providential result that materialized at this time involved a dignified young woman named, symbolically enough, Mary Ann Angell. Mary Ann had "gathered" at Kirtland in the spring of 1833. Thus she was already there by the time Brigham and his daughters and Heber Kimball and his family arrived about six months later in September. Mary Ann had been born in Seneca, in Ontario County, New York, not far from Mendon, but she had been working in Providence, Rhode Island, three years earlier when she heard Elder Thomas B. Marsh preach on *The Book of Mormon*. She obtained a copy from him and was so taken with its revelations that she underwent a strong spiritual transformation and returned home in 1832 to Ontario County to be nearer the source of this new religion.

Back in New York, she soon met Joseph, Phineas, and Lorenzo Young. They reinforced her faith in *The Book of Mormon* and its teachings. Before long, Mary Ann had passed the book along to her parents, who also found it spiritually moving and full of truth. As a result, she and her parents were baptized as Saints by Brigham's brother-in-law John P. Greene, Rhoda's husband. When the three Young brothers, Rhoda, and her husband John left for Kirtland shortly thereafter, Mary Ann made plans to move there as well. In Kirtland she was quite taken with Brigham's preaching, and he in turn was moved when he heard her attest to the strength and depth of her new faith.

By this time Brigham had been grieving Miriam's death for a full year, and he had concerns that he and his daughters were presuming on the kindness and hospitality of the Kimballs—even though Vilate Kimball looked upon Brigham's daughters as though they were her own, and not just the children of her best friend. He may have had fears of losing yet another woman he loved and cherished, but by now Brigham was no doubt immersed in loneliness and longing for a companion to share his cares and hopes. The "gritty" Brigham, as he would one day describe himself in writing, had the fortitude to risk all in love again. Perhaps he felt the risk was worth it, especially for marriage with a woman as devout as Mary Ann.

The two married on February 10, 1834. They would prove to be a powerful couple with enormous influence on the Mormon community in Kirtland and later on the Mormon communities in Missouri, Illinois, and Utah. Mary Ann exhibited enthusiasm and fervor in caring for Brigham's daughters, in providing him with a loving home, and in her devout faith as a Saint.

Her support was important because by now Brigham was no longer unnoticed among the more senior members of the Mormon community.

His great talents for organization and leadership had become evident. Joseph Smith was highly impressed with the way Brigham had conducted himself in Kirtland. Brigham's preaching was first-rate and his work in the community was generously offered and equally excellent. Smith had told his followers of his plans to build a temple in Kirtland and also to establish a kind of seminary there—what he called the "School for the Elders"—and Brigham's talents were greatly needed.

Yet before plans for building a model community in Kirtland could be carried out, problems erupted elsewhere. From their very beginnings, Mormons had been subject to random harassment and even violence. Joseph Smith had suffered much legal harassment and many threats to his life; once he had even been tarred and feathered by a mob wishing to drive him out of town. Such unchristian behavior was not news to Brigham. As early as the spring of 1832, shortly after he and his family had organized the branch of the new church in Mendon, and the congregation of Latter-day Saints gathered for a prayer service in a barn in Victor, near where Joseph Young lived, no sooner had the service begun than a mob stormed the barn and besieged the congregation until the Saints had no choice but to disperse.

According to Brigham's own account, the new Mendon branch had not yet foregathered three times before they were attacked in this way. Their enemies attributed every sort of depravity falsely to the Saints. They were accused of "stripping stark naked" and of then having the "holy roll." None of these wild accusations was true, but the Saints often found themselves challenged by members of long-established religious denominations, who would quite frequently incite the local political and legal authorities to step in and stop the Saints from conducting their services, sometimes dispersing them by force.

What hurt the Mormons' plans to build the ideal community at Kirtland was an outbreak of strife in Missouri. When Brigham had been married to Mary Ann only a matter of weeks, Joseph Smith became alarmed at the violence being visited on the community of Saints he had dispatched to Missouri to establish the new religion on what was then the westernmost settled boundary of the United States. In the all ready well-established missionary tradition of the Saints, Smith had hoped to convert both the new settlers in Missouri and the indigenous peoples. He had called for the Saints to set up a central gathering place in Jackson County, Missouri. By the fall of 1833, there were twelve hundred Saints there, two hundred more than were in Kirtland. Many of these Missouri Mormons had previously settled in or passed through Kirtland. At Smith's behest they had forged a way farther west, seeking to fulfill his wish to found a Zion in Jackson County, a new "City of God."

On February 24, 1834, Smith had a revelation about the situation in Missouri. The community of Saints there had suffered the depredations that mobocracy usually visits on the underdog or the outsider. Mormons were both. There had been beatings and vandalism of their property, including the smashing of a printing press. Legal harassment had also been visited upon them. Then, suddenly, serious violence erupted against them in Independence. The bishop of the Mormon community there was tarred and feathered. Mormon homes were burned after their residents were hauled outside and beaten; what's more, the mob had confiscated much of their furniture and carted it away before torching the houses. When the Saints complained to Governor Daniel Dunklin, he at first said he needed a posse of Saints to assist him to restore order. Then, suddenly, he washed his hands of the whole travesty in the face of a rising tide of hostility from the locals.

In the vision Joseph Smith had, he saw the need to send an army of Saints to reinforce and save the Mormons in Missouri. Spreading this message among his followers, Smith appealed to Brigham to join the force—called "Zion's Camp" by Smith—that was heading to Missouri. Smith had noted Brigham's outstanding organizational abilities and talent for leadership, as well as his many other skills. Brigham immediately volunteered to go. His brother Joseph was another matter. It took a chance meeting with Smith, at which Brigham was also present, before Joseph agreed to undertake this daunting task with Smith and Brigham and about two hundred others.

While Brigham would be away in Missouri, he could leave his two daughters in the care of their stepmother, Mary Ann. She was also asked to help with her brother Solomon's family, since Solomon was adamant that he also wanted to go to Missouri and help out. Solomon Angell's friend Lorenzo Booth, too, joined the force headed to Missouri, and Mary Ann graciously agreed to look after his family as well—despite being pregnant with her first child.

Zion's Camp was not a haphazard undertaking. Joseph Smith proved his leadership mettle yet again, organizing a force of about sixteen units composed of twelve men each. Each unit had a captain selected by the men in the unit. Brigham was chosen as a captain, as was Heber Kimball. In each unit the men were assigned tasks: two to build and tend the fires, two to cook, two to pitch and strike the tents and tend to the bedding, two to fetch water, two to attend to the horses, and one to do the running of chores and errands and communiqués among the wagons. The overall executive responsibility was the captain's. He had to see that everything ran efficiently and that order prevailed. The men making this journey had each acquired a gun with bayonet, a hunting knife, powder, and shot. Smith had expended much energy in amassing twenty-five baggage wagons loaded with arms, provisions, and tools and farming supplies needed in Missouri. He intended to bring the Missouri Saints relief and to preserve the community they had set up.

In the first week of May, after two months of planning, organization, and provisioning, the wagon train called Zion's Camp pulled out of Kirtland headed for Jackson County, Missouri, a thousand difficult miles away.

CHAPTER 7

ZION'S CAMP

In the Mormon belief system, nothing happens that is not part of God's master plan. Nothing occurs without a larger purpose. Brigham Young believed this fervently, and his backbreaking journey to Missouri as a captain with Joseph Smith's Zion's Camp confirmed in his mind that what happened was meant to be. It was, in effect, a trial run for the great role of American Moses that Brigham would later play in the Mormon exodus to the desert kingdom in the Far West. The chance to observe and learn from Joseph Smith presented itself to Brigham as a captain in Zion's Camp every single day. The leadership ability Brigham saw in Smith indelibly stamped his own style of leadership later: Brigham would be firm but flexible, vigilant but able to relax discipline when necessary, encouraging but capable of a mild rebuke, stalwart and uncomplaining but never above sympathy and compassion. From studying Joseph Smith, Brigham learned not just to lead but to inspire. He learned the importance of mentoring through example. Whatever hardships had to be borne, he bore nobly, as he observed Smith do. Brigham learned to push toward the goal but to allow for a respite when exhaustion and privation threatened his people and came near to breaking their will.

The suffering and difficulties faced by the members of Zion's Camp are now lore and legend among the Latter-day Saints, and they deserve to be. For one thing, the men had to live off the land. Each unit of twelve men had to forage, hunt, trap, and fish each day for their meals. They could not possibly have brought along a ready food supply for themselves and at the same time hauled the provisions, equipment, supplies, and tools needed to relieve the beleaguered Missouri community. The terrain they crossed was brutal, scarcely charted, let alone cleared and smoothed. Many times the men had to combine their strength to haul a supply wagon up an especially steep hill or to propel it across a swift-running and muddy stream or brook. Sometimes it was necessary for thirty men to heave and haul a single wagon. Since almost the entire thousand miles had to be negotiated on foot, the men who developed painful blisters or other debilitating foot ailments sometimes had to ride in the crude, uncomfortable wagons, none of the which had springs, so the men were tossed about roughly. Along the way nearly everyone's feet bled profusely. Joseph Young said he could hear the blood sloshing in his boots as he trudged along.

Brigham watched and learned when Smith diplomatically handled local authorities as the wagon train passed through the scattered settlements on the western frontier. Often the locals were hostile and threatening, and Smith had to use gentleness and persuasion to assure the local leaders that he and his people were peaceful and merely passing through. Mormons could set off quite severe paranoia in members of more established sects such as the Baptists and the Methodists. Smith wanted to be careful not to incite any increased hostility against his people. There was already so much suspicion of the Saints and so much falsehood spread about them. He wanted no impediments to get in the way of the purpose of the journey—to reach the suffering community of Missouri Saints and relieve them.

The Midwestern heat that spring of 1834 was oppressive, and in addition to all the sores and suffering inherent in hiking so far on foot, there was the horrible problem of mosquitoes attacking them at night. Brigham wrote of the rigors of this journey. His duties were such that he rarely lay down to sleep before eleven or twelve at night—and the bell sounded at 3:00 a.m. to wake the men and warn them to prepare to eat, strike camp, and move on. Most of the men were making this long trek on three or four hours of sleep per night, footsore, exhausted, and under attack from swarms of mosquitoes. Though they were uncomplaining men, both Smith and Brigham singled out the mosquitoes as especially annoying in their written recollections of Zion's Camp.

The members of Zion's Camp were sustained along the way by their faith. To arrive in Missouri within a month, the wagon train had to average nearly thirty-five miles per day. Almost every man had to cover this distance while carrying twenty or so pounds of personal equipment on his back: rifle, knife, powder, shot, a few spare pieces of clothing, and a few items necessary for hygiene. The relief must have been great each evening when the men knew they had traversed the required mileage and they could stop for the night. After they had attended to setting up camp and eating a meal, the entire contingent would meet for singing and prayer, which together fortified their spirit and increased their resolve. Sometimes these prayer sessions drew the interest of locals, a number of whom were so impressed they asked to join the wagon train and learn more about this new religion. The Saints accommodated their wish and took along a handful of potential converts, including women and children who, if old enough, helped out with the cooking and the serving of meals.

So many difficulties were encountered along the way that Brigham became annoyed with the constant complainers. But Smith counseled him to forebear and not to strike out at these unfortunate souls. These malcontents, dubbed "Zion's Scamps" by Brigham, had started to complain about befouled water and spoiled and stale bread and cheese, about butter that had started to turn, and about bacon and other foodstuffs infested with maggots. They also whined about their blistered heels and sore toes. When confronted with the long litany of complaints, Smith exhibited outstanding patience and treated the discontented as he would have treated overtired children. He listened, he sympathized, he coaxed them onward, and—most important—he refrained from criticizing them.

Naturally, complaining increased toward the end of the long trip, as physical ailments and exhaustion intensified. Yet Smith himself never complained, setting a stout and inspiring example for one and all. Once the wagon train had crossed the western boundary of Indiana, the men encountered more difficulty in obtaining baked bread and other dietary staples because settlements now became scarce. Instead they had to seek basic ingredients, like flour, and make their own bread, corn bread, and corn dodgers, a kind of primitive bread stick made by frying or baking cornmeal.

But these were minor problems compared to what happened next. As the wagon train drew near Missouri, Smith sent Orson Hyde and Parley P. Pratt ahead to contact the Saints in Jefferson City and to meet with Governor Dunklin and confirm that they could still count on his help, now that a posse of Saints would soon be on the spot. That's when Governor Dunklin pulled the double cross mentioned earlier. Claiming that he had underestimated the amount of resistance to the Saints' colonizing in Missouri, and further that he feared civil war would break out if he aided the Mormons, the governor reversed himself and said he could not help. The whole tense situation came to a head on June 16 in a courthouse in Liberty, Clay County, Missouri. Hostility to the Mormons ran high. Matters became so heated at one point that bloodshed threatened to break out. The Saints were going to find it extremely difficult to reclaim their land and possessions in Missouri.

Nevertheless, Smith led his troop of followers on toward Jackson County, even as violence threatened to erupt with every mile they travelled. As the sun set on the evening of June 19, 1834, a party of five men rode into Zion's encampment and informed Smith that a band of as many as 130 mounted and heavily armed men had sworn to attack the camp that very night and wipe out the entire traveling party of Mormons. Written testimony has been left of what happened next: a thrashing storm with hail the size of walnuts and torrential squalls of rain moved in rapidly and lashed the earth and everything on it.

Several Saints said they had seen violent and frightening storms but never one as intense and paralyzing as the one that descended upon them that night. The Saints clustered in a large lodge fashioned from logs and watched in open-mouthed awe throughout the storm. Only when it eased, what seemed hours later, did they realize that their enemies would be unable to reach them that night. Later the Saints learned that the attacking party had been so fiercely battered by hail that it had left holes in their hats and broken the stocks off their rifles. The downpour flooded streams and rivers, and the would-be raiders' horses threw them to the ground in panic. Heber Kimball later said that it was obvious that God had come to the defense of the Saints.

The morning after the storm, Zion's Camp had an important visitor. A Colonel John Sconce of the Missouri militia and two other militiamen of Ray County, which the colonel called home, came to speak with the Saints about their plans. Smith spoke to the three men and convinced them the intentions of the Saints were benign. He explained to the important visitors how the Mormons had suffered from prejudice and misunderstanding and from unfounded fears incited by wild and ridiculous rumors. So impressed were the colonel and his two companions that they promised to try to allay the fears of the local Missourians and to aid the Mormons in achieving their peaceful goal to come to the aid of their Missouri community.

But this was not to be. On the very day the colonel and his two companions visited, cholera struck Zion's Camp. Three Saints fell ill that day, and soon there was a small epidemic. Smith did his best to quickly travel farther west in hopes of reaching the community of beleaguered Saints they had come to relieve, but the mission got no closer than five or six miles before they were intercepted by a small military unit under the direction of General Clyde B. Atchison of the Missouri militia. Atchison told them that anti-Mormon feelings were raging among the locals and that it would be impossible for Smith and his followers to get any closer to the settlement of Saints without bloodletting breaking out. Atchison pleaded with Smith to turn his wagon train around. In the end, Smith felt there was no choice left to him. With no other viable option available, Zion's Camp set up camp for the night in the field of a fellow Saint named Brother Burket.

There and then, the cholera erupted again with a vengeance, with deadly results over the next two weeks. In all, sixty-eight members of Zion's Camp fell ill with cholera and fourteen perished. For the days the dreadful sickness ravaged the encampment, the men were besieged and distraught. Then they faced the sad task of burying the deceased. This they did under cover of night. Having no coffins and no lumber to fashion them—and no time, since violence still threatened—the survivors wrapped the dead in blankets and laid them to their rest on a small rise near Rush Creek on the border of Brother Burket's property.

Heber Kimball had contracted the disease but fought it off with all his strength and faith. Neither Brigham nor his brother Joseph succumbed to cholera. Nor did Joseph Smith. When the disease had killed fourteen members of the group, Smith drew the men together and told them if they committed themselves fully to honor and obey the laws of their covenant with the Lord, the plague would pass over and they would be spared further affliction. The men raised their hands and testified that from that moment on they would honor their covenant with God as conveyed by his servant Joseph Smith, and the cholera outbreak did abate.

On July 3, Smith called everyone together and officially disbanded Zion's Camp. The men were free to stay in Missouri or to travel back to Kirtland. He told them Zion had not been attained this time but that it would be later. Brigham and Joseph Young set out the very next morning with Heber Kimball and several of the brethren to return to Kirtland and their families. They walked the entire distance through the savage midsummer heat. Again they hazarded the hardships of providing food for themselves and endured swarms of mosquitoes. Again their feet suffered. Yet their high level of motivation for the journey was clear—they arrived back in Kirtland in early August, having averaged about forty miles a day.

For the rest of his life, Brigham saw this whole aborted and failed mission in a positive light. And he had good reason for doing so. He treasured the experience of traveling under the direction of Joseph Smith. Brigham had learned numerous lessons from Smith about organizing, planning, and executing a long and arduous march, and he also gleaned insights from watching Smith handle and motivate people. Brigham had learned lessons in diplomacy and wisdom, too, in handling potentially violent mobs intent on harming Mormons. These precious lessons would stand Brigham in good stead for the rest of his life; he would rely on the experience and Smith's example years later to lead the Saints to the Zion they achieved when they established their church and community in Salt Lake City—and helped colonize the West.

CHAPTER 8

THE QUORUM
OF
TWELVE

The failure of Zion's Camp was a setback for the Saints. But Joseph Smith—like Brigham Young—always saw opportunity in failure. When the survivors returned to Kirtland, there was but a slight lull in spirits during the autumn of 1834. During this time Brigham hastily used his skills to acquire needed groceries, clothing, and other supplies for his family. He had returned flat broke from the trek to Missouri. In the time he was away Mary Ann, though pregnant, had struggled and kept the household afloat. Then, in October, she delivered her first child and Brigham's third, a son they named Joseph Angell Young, the first name in honor of the prophet. Positive as ever in his thinking and his vision, Smith spent the autumn thinking how best to carry out the mission of the church in the future. Five years earlier he had experienced a revelation in which he was directed to institute the Quorum of Twelve Apostles. The time to do so was now upon him.

On Sunday, February 8, 1835, following the morning services, Smith asked Brigham and Joseph Young to come to his home that afternoon and sing for him. The Young brothers possessed harmonious voices and often sang in prayer circles and in preaching sessions. That afternoon's singing session proved to be both cathartic and momentous for the Latter-day Saints. After the Youngs sang, they prayed with Smith, and then he reminisced about the vicissitudes and setbacks of Zion's Camp. He especially bemoaned the lives of the faithful lost to the cholera out-break. All three men commiserated together, and then Smith said that he wished only to achieve the heavenly rest that had been bestowed by the Lord on those who had succumbed to the disease. At this statement he was greatly moved and began to relate the revelation he had experi-enced five years earlier instructing him to establish the Quorum of Twelve Apostles.

While the Young brothers had been singing for what Brigham later stated was "a long time," Smith had been receiving another revelation, a simple one: those who had shown themselves steadfast should form the majority of the Twelve Apostles. In other words, Zion's Camp had been the crucible in which the majority of the Twelve Apostles had been formed. Those who had shown their mettle during that trial by fire, Smith believed, were qualified to lead the faithful forward and to preach the new gospel far and wide, even into foreign lands, where nations were shrouded in darkness. Before the Young brothers left that day, Smith instructed Brigham that he was the messenger chosen to deliver the message about the anointment of the Apostles. He told Brigham to instruct the brethren living within a reasonable traveling distance to come to a general confer-ence in six days, on Saturday, February 14, 1835. There the prophet would anoint the Twelve Apostles whose assignment it would be to spread the gospel far and wide in the missionary tradition of the Saints.

That Saturday evening was memorable. The number gathered for the conference was substantial. When they entered the meeting hall,

Smith immediately directed the survivors of Zion's Camp to sit in a
section reserved exclusively for them. Next, he recounted in graphic
detail the hardships endured and the trouble overcome on this momentous, though failed, mission. He lavishly praised the men who had shown
themselves to be stouthearted and uncomplaining throughout the worst
days of this ordeal. He recounted how he had received a revelation and
a vision five years earlier to designate a Quorum of Twelve Apostles. Only
last week, he added, a further divine intervention had alerted him that
the brave, devout, and courageous men of Zion's Camp should form the
Quorum's backbone and constitute its majority. Because of that intervention from the Holy Spirit, Smith stated that he now felt comfortable
forming the Quorum.

In selecting the Quorum's members, Smith announced that he had
enlisted the help of the Three Witnesses: Oliver Cowdery, David Whitmer, and Martin Harris. These were designated witnesses because they
had been shown the gold plates revealed by the angel Moroni, the very
plates that Smith had translated into *The Book of Mormon*. The Three
Witnesses then executed a laying-on of hands on each man selected to
be ordained to the priesthood and known thereafter as an Apostle and
a member of the Quorum of Twelve Apostles. By becoming Apostles,
these dozen men were vested with special priestly powers to go forth and
preach and heal, and to spread the new gospel. Adding to the solemnity
of the proceedings, the members of the First Presidency, a supreme
executive council, would also execute a laying-on of hands on the twelve
men selected.

The First Presidency members were Joseph Smith, Sidney Rigdon,
and Frederick G. Williams. After the dual ceremonies of the laying-on
of hands, one final act of investiture remained: Oliver Cowdery addressed
the Twelve Apostles directly about the responsibilities now incumbent
upon them. Cowdery's role in the commissioning of the Twelve Apostles
was significant because, like Joseph Smith, Oliver Cowdery had been

given the powers of the Aaronic priesthood by John the Baptist and the powers of the Melchizedek priesthood by Peter, James, and John, three of the Lord's Apostles. Cowdery emphasized to the selected Apostles that their mandate was to preach the new gospel.

And the Twelve Apostles wasted very little time in carrying out that mandate, setting off very soon for a missionary sweep through New York State and parts of New England. The twelve men selected were Thomas B. Marsh, David W. Patten, Brigham Young, Heber Chase Kimball, Orson Hyde, William E. McLellin, Parley P. Pratt, Luke S. Johnson, William Smith, Orson Pratt, John F. Boynton, and Lyman E. Johnson. Of these twelve, only Marsh, Boynton, and McLellin had not been members of Zion's Camp. Note that Thomas B. Marsh is the same man who had converted Brigham's second wife Mary Ann Angell back in Rhode Island, and that David W. Patten had been converted by Brigham on one of his early missionary junkets into western New York State and Ontario shortly after first meeting Smith in Kirtland a few months after Brigham's own conversion. The early Saints were a tightly welded community of devout believers. Yet over time this unity would be challenged—as is inevitable in any organization—by the stresses and strains of group dynamics.

But for now the Quorum of Twelve was exulting in their ordination and wasting no time in carrying out their mission. Smith explained that the Twelve Apostles should act in concert as a group. He told them they should appoint one of their number to preside over each meeting and, further, that they should have a secretary and someone appointed to take minutes at each meeting. Even when their missionary callings separated them by great distances, they should know one another's whereabouts and keep in touch as much as possible. On top of these instructions, the Apostles took seriously the fiery rhetoric of Oliver Cowdery, the assistant president of the church, who had charged them with the duty to proselytize. Cowdery had told them that though their lives would sometimes be in danger they would possess great powers to heal the sick, cast out devils, raise the dead, and open the eyes of the blind, among other priestly gifts. They were to go forth from land to land and from sea to sea to exercise such powers and gain new converts. Yet another task laid on them was that of acquiring funds to buy land for new settlements of Saints.

The Quorum of Twelve immediately devised an agenda and set out to fulfill it. This agenda, completed by the end of March 1835, called for a start date of May 4 of the same year. The Apostles would travel back east and fan out over New York State, most of New England, and vast tracts of Ontario. They would travel and preach and convert and collect the means to acquire land to establish new branches of the church. Not one of the new Apostles set out with more determination and fervor than did Brigham. He was his usual devout and enthusiastic self— naturally dismayed when he had to return briefly to Kirtland in June to bear witness at a trial. A discontented member of Zion's Camp had brought suit against Smith for breach of promise, claiming that Smith had failed to deliver on a promised "plot" in Missouri. When called to the stand and questioned, Brigham said that the only plot he knew to be promised to anyone was in a cemetery, generally of six feet. In the end, the plaintiff, Denis Lake, lost the case. Brigham, wasting no time, immediately set out for the east to resume his missionary work.

Although Brigham met mainly with success on his first mission as an Apostle, he did experience setbacks and harsh rejections as well, even one from a relative in western New York State who adamantly refused to convert no matter how fervently Brigham exhorted him. But to balance the scales, Brigham did experience another encounter with family that was quite edifying. In late August and early September, he was preaching in and around Boston, and he decided to divert his steps to Hopkinton to visit the Howes, relatives on his mother's side of the family. Brigham's Howe grandmother was especially pleased to see one of her long-dead daughter Abigail's children. The meeting also brought palpable joy to Brigham.

Brigham's mission ended shortly thereafter, and he started back to Kirtland and arrived on September 26, 1835. Brigham calculated that during this excursion he averaged twenty miles a day and totaled 3,264 miles. As before, most of this distance was covered on foot, with only an occasional wagon or boat ride to speed him along and break the monotony. Again, Brigham had travelled light and received most of his shelter and board in the homes of established Saints or of his new converts. When he got back to Kirtland, he was relieved to find that, in his absence, Mary Ann had managed well, new son and all. Encouraged by the success of his first mission as an Apostle, Brigham was convinced more than ever that he had a calling to answer and a destiny to fulfill.

CHAPTER 9

THE TEMPLE
— AND THE —
TEMPEST

For the six months after Brigham returned to Kirtland, he mixed his duties as an Apostle charged to preach the new gospel with another preoccupation he had acquired as a loyal and devoted follower of Joseph Smith. The centerpiece of the Saints' first headquarters there was the first LDS temple, built under Smith's direction. With his many artisan skills, Brigham played a key role in the construction of the temple. The building project preoccupied him, and his assiduity in helping organize and build the temple further ingratiated him to Smith. As an accomplished carpenter and furniture-maker, Brigham undertook supervision of the interior woodwork of the building—the pews, the pulpits, the doorjambs, and the window frames. With the windows, his skills as a glazier came into play.

The Kirtland temple still stands today, a tasteful example of late Federalist architecture, with a large pediment above a well-proportioned three-story façade. At the center of the pediment is a large oval window, and above and behind the pediment rises a tower topped with a domed cupola whose sides hold decorative gothic windows. The masonry is striking; it glistens with a sheen imparted by the pieces of china the women contributed to be pulverized and mixed with the plaster. Sidney Rigdon supervised this outstanding plasterwork while Smith oversaw the stonecutting. As the temple neared completion, Brigham took charge of the painting and finishing work. His innate leadership and organizational talents, combined with his vast experience as a builder, came to the fore as he supervised this final phase of construction.

After several years of construction, the temple stood complete, and Smith dedicated and consecrated it in March of 1836. For four days straight, all the men remained inside—conducting services, praying, singing, fasting, anointing, and washing. Smith considered the washing of feet commanded by Jesus to be an essential sacred ritual. As the four days of worship drew to a close, Smith and Oliver Cowdery sat behind a veil at the front of the temple. When the veil was finally lifted, Smith confided to the congregation that the Lord had appeared to him and to Cowdery, as had Moses, Elijah, and Elias. Heber Kimball later added that he had seen a very tall personage hovering above the veil, an angel with black eyes and white hair, dressed in a long gown and shod in sandals. The angel, Kimball said, had been sent as a messenger to sanctify the dedication. Smith had long promised that upon completion and dedication the temple would impart a spiritual endowment to the Saints, and many later testified that they felt this heavenly sense of exhilaration.

The temple fulfilled a dream for Smith. He conceived of it as serving three main functions. First, it was a sacred house of worship where the Saints could practice their faith and embrace their God. Second, the upper floor served as a seminary; it housed the "School of the Elders" that had been envisioned by Smith years earlier. There Smith and his associates taught the Apostles and the elders the principles of the new gospel and instructed them in how to preach *The Book of Mormon*. Smith also instituted secular classes on the upper floor and even brought in a non-Mormon teacher of Hebrew. Some of the secular classes taught basic grammar school subjects and so increased the level of education and literacy among the Saints. Third, the temple housed the central administrative office for the church. Smith himself had a suite of offices on the upper floor, complete with a staff of secretaries and other clerical workers.

The completion and opening of the temple represented a huge milestone for Smith and for all the Saints, but there were ominous developments in the offing. The lawsuit brought by Denis Lake, the member of Zion's Camp disappointed not to have received what he claimed was a promised plot of land in Missouri, served as a kind of prototype of other grievances soon raised against Smith and his chief colleagues. In the fall of 1836, several members of the Quorum of Twelve Apostles, plus the three witnesses to *The Book of Mormon*, in league with a handful of other influential Saints, attempted a coup against Joseph Smith's leadership. They sought to replace Smith as head of the church with David Whitmer, one of the witnesses. There was a growing feeling within the higher echelons of the church that Smith was too involved in temporal matters better left to others. The disaffected members thought that as a prophet Smith should confine himself to spiritual and theological matters and leave business and finance to other members of the church better suited to handle them.

Brigham viewed the attempted coup with horror and denounced it as heresy. Joseph Smith's father and Heber Chase Kimball agreed with Brigham. And Brigham's denunciation of this insurrection reinforced his reputation for assertive rhetoric. He argued that disrespectful talk and usurpation of Smith's rightful role as head of the church would wreck the authority of those sponsoring the change and lead them straight to hell. One of Joseph Smith's enemies was an old boxer named

Jacob Bump. As Brigham denounced the coup, Bump lunged at him, shouting that he could not keep his hands off him. Ignoring Bump, Brigham calmly stated that the whole affair was an abomination. Fearing that the rebellious faction might kill Joseph Smith, Brigham and Smith's brother William drove a wagon to the outskirts of town and intercepted a stagecoach bringing Smith back to Kirtland. William took his brother's place in the stagecoach, and Brigham slipped back into town quietly with Joseph Smith as his passenger.

Next, a man named Hawley showed up in Kirtland from New York State, claiming he had certain knowledge that the Lord had rejected Joseph Smith. The man had walked barefoot to Kirtland to inform Smith of his rejection, which Hawley said had been made known to him in a vision while he was out plowing a field on his New York property. Undaunted, Hawley caused havoc for several days by walking down the center of the town's streets and denouncing Joseph Smith at the top of his lungs at night, warning that the inhabitants of the town would meet with perdition if they did not expel Smith as a false prophet. Hawley's behavior so riled Brigham that one night he rose from his bed, jumped into his clothes, pulled on his boots, and went out and threatened to thrash Hawley with a cowhide whip. Brigham shouted at Hawley to cease and desist because they had the Lord's prophet in their midst, and they didn't need a prophet from the devil like him. Apparently Brigham scared Hawley enough that he left off raising a ruckus and disappeared.

That fall of 1836, one threat to the Saints appeared after another. The Saints had almost always had contentious relations with the civil authorities wherever they settled. Kirtland proved no different. Joseph Smith had empowered many elders to perform the marriage ceremony. Before too long, knowledge of this practice spread beyond Kirtland and came to the attention of the civil authorities in the county seat. They convened a grand jury that indicted Joseph Smith, his father, and his

younger brother Don Carlos Smith. Found guilty, all three men were
fined a thousand dollars apiece for performing marriage ceremonies
without legal sanction. Yet these legal problems over matrimonial
matters paled in comparison to what would happen the following year.

In 1837, the booming United States economy crashed. For years there
had been rampant speculation in land and a proliferation in the number
of banks, bringing the total number of banks in the country to 850.
Before the year was out roughly half of these banks failed, precipitating
the crash of 1837, the worst economic crisis for the United States in the
entirety of the nineteenth century. Joseph Smith had been avid to cash
in on the boom that led to the bust. He had borrowed ninety thousand
dollars in 1836 alone. This may well have been the underlying reason
behind the aborted coup to oust Smith—lack of confidence in Smith's
business acumen. In November of 1836, Smith received a revelation
instructing him to found a bank with cash reserves of four million
dollars. The Kirtland Safety Society Bank soon opened, under the
presidency of Sidney Rigdon, and with Smith as cashier.

Since coming to Kirtland, Smith had been allied with Democratic
politicians; he had delivered the Mormon vote to them in many elections.
This did not sit well with the opposing Whig Party. In retaliation, the
Whigs in the state senate denied the new Mormon bank a charter late
in December of 1836, only a month after the bank came into existence.
The Saints then took evasive action. They had already printed up the
new bank's notes, so they simply altered them by inserting *anti* before
the word "bank" and adding *ing* after it. Their former bank was now
called the Kirtland Safety Society Anti-Banking Company. Many high-
ranking church officials and other prominent Kirtland Mormons had
signed the incorporation papers of this institution, binding themselves
over to one another and specifying a one-hundred-thousand-dollar
penalty for reneging on the agreement. Brigham, Joseph, and Lorenzo
Dow Young had signed this liability document.

The bank was heavily overleveraged. Smith and Rigdon had bought three thousand shares apiece at par value of fifty dollars per share. Smith's wife Emma bought twelve hundred shares. Joseph Young and Heber Chase Kimball took a thousand each. Brigham purchased two thousand shares on December 9, 1836, with a scanty down payment of only seven dollars in cash. Hardly any collateral underpinned the new "anti-bank" except for homes and small amounts of cash.

Using their powerful press connections, the Whigs set to work quickly to undermine this latest Mormon enterprise. The Cleveland *Gazette* and the Plainesville *Telegraph* ran articles casting aspersions on the solvency of the Kirtland Safety Society Anti-Banking Company. The anti-bank's notes plummeted in value. Two weeks after being issued, the notes had lost 87 percent of their par value. Total disaster struck when the economic crash came along in the spring of 1837.

Long-established and reputable banks failed in New York, Boston, Philadelphia, and other large commercial cities on the eastern seaboard. This put the Saints behind the eight ball. Rigdon transferred his property to his daughter, and Brigham signed over six hundred dollars worth of land to Mary Ann's father. In a last-ditch effort to reverse the bank's impending financial collapse, Smith dispatched the Twelve Apostles to distant cities where the bank's notes were still being accepted. In August, while Smith preached in Canada, Brigham swept through his old stomping grounds in western and central New York State. There he was able to sell forty thousand dollars worth of notes that had lost virtually all value. According to some sources, writs were issued for Brigham's arrest, but he returned to Kirtland intact.

In Kirtland things were not good. Most of the high-ranking church officials had been implicated in the anti-banking scheme. Lawsuits proliferated. Several large court settlements and out-of-court settlements followed. Worse was the dissension that erupted within the church. In September three of the Twelve Apostles—John F. Boynton, Luke Johnson, and Lyman E. Johnson—denounced Joseph Smith as a fraud. They were excommunicated at a church meeting where Brigham railed against Boynton and told him face to face that he must repent of his sins.

Matters heated up from that point on. Shortly thereafter, as Joseph Smith's father preached from the pulpit in the temple on Sunday, Boynton and other church dissidents stormed in and shouted for Father Smith to stop denouncing them. Boynton and his followers were armed. When the prophet's brother William attempted to shield his father from Boynton's wrath, Boynton threatened to impale him on a sword. One of Boynton's group of angry dissidents was Joseph Smith's secretary, Warren Parrish. Boynton and two of his cohorts eventually sued Smith and Rigdon and received nearly three thousand dollars in damages from the court. For the rest of his life, Boynton remained a severe critic of Mormonism, characterizing it as "humbug."

The Mormon community at Kirtland was hopelessly fractured. To settle judgments against the church stemming from the bank scandal, the temple—which had cost forty thousand dollars to build—was sold at auction for $150. The shop housing the printing press where the infamous bank notes had been printed burned to the ground the night before its scheduled turnover in payment of another court judgment handed down against Smith and Rigdon. On the morning of December 22, 1837, Brigham had to flee Kirtland under cover of dark to avoid his creditors. And three weeks later, on January 12, 1838, Smith and Rigdon took flight for the same reason.

Official Mormon history maintains that Smith, Brigham, and Rigdon fled to avoid the violence of the "apostates," as Boynton and the other dissidents came to be called. The truth is that the banking scandal had visited ruin upon Smith and many upper-echelon Mormons in Ohio, including Brigham and Rigdon. A month after these three nearly ruined men had to take flight on horseback by night, Warren Parrish detailed in the Plainesville *Republican*—in a letter also vouched for by Boynton and Luke Johnson—how the banking scheme had been a financial bubble right from the start, lacking proper capitalization. Parrish also asserted that Smith had ordered the printing press burned to the ground, so that it could not be used to denounce him. The newspaper offered to publish any signed rebuttal to Parrish's letter, but none ever came. Today, Parrish's name has been blackened in some official Mormon histories, but it seems clear that he does not deserve such treatment. In this banking enterprise, Joseph Smith went overboard—he fell victim to misplaced optimism, as did many other Americans. He speculated recklessly. But he also seems to have acted dishonestly. And in this instance Brigham's loyalty cost him, involving him in foolish speculation with little collateral—and possibly in fraud.

This bleak period in the winter of 1838 marked the nadir of the history of the Latter-day Saints to that point. But later, in Utah, their church would be troubled again with allegations of financial irregularities, favoritism, and bullying. Brigham had his detractors, sometimes even among the Saints, when it came to his sharp business practices.

CHAPTER 10

BACK
• TO •
MISSOURI

After Brigham sneaked out of Kirtland under cover of night three days before Christmas 1837, he rode on a southwesterly bias to rendezvous with his brother Lorenzo Dow in Dublin, Indiana, a small town just to the west of the Ohio state line. Lorenzo was wintering in Dublin on his way to Missouri. Less than a month after Brigham arrived in Dublin, Joseph Smith and Sidney Rigdon rode into town. They, too, had decided to try to reach the large community of Saints who were still in Missouri even though Zion's Camp had been routed years earlier in its mission to liberate and stabilize the Mormon communities in that state. The immediate problem for Smith was money. He had none, not even enough to make the trip to Missouri. At first he attempted to earn the funds for the trip by sawing logs and chopping wood alongside Brigham and Sidney. But the pay from this work was not sufficient to bring in the amount of money he needed.

In a surprise move, Smith turned to Brigham for advice. Taken aback by this role reversal, Brigham at first was unsure what to say. Then, when he realized that Smith was in earnest, Brigham told him to rest for the journey and assured him he would have the needed funds soon. As it turned out, Brigham was at that time advising a man named Tomlinson on the sale of his farm. When the sale went through, Brigham counseled Tomlinson, a fellow Mormon, to advance Smith enough money to make his journey to Missouri, where Smith had long since declared that the church should establish its headquarters and build the new Zion. Tomlinson agreed and gave Smith three hundred dollars. This was more than enough to get Smith and Rigdon to Missouri. Smith and Rigdon set out several days later.

Shortly thereafter, Brigham decided to join them. He caught up with them at Quincy, Illinois. The three then traveled the last two hundred miles together and arrived in Far West, Missouri, on March 14, 1838. After the failure of the Zion's Camp attempt to save the Saints threatened with expulsion from Jackson County, the Missouri Saints had moved one county north, across the Missouri River to Clay County. But Clay County proved untenable for Mormon settlement as well, and the still substantial community of Saints in Missouri had moved to Caldwell, the county northeast of Clay. There they colonized the town of Far West, which eventually became the Caldwell county seat. But even in Far West, all was not well.

Brigham Young, steadfast as ever, had followed Smith and Rigdon to Far West despite his misgivings about Missouri. Brigham knew that, years earlier, shortly after Smith founded his church in 1830, he had declared Independence, Missouri, the site of the new Zion. Church headquarters were to be established and the main temple built there. These plans had all come crashing down when Zion's Camp failed and the Mormons were forced from Jackson County by the local authorities. Ever since then Brigham had been wary of Missouri. The state had many substantial people in it, but it was also wide open and full of freebooters and criminals. Lawlessness was always a threat. Loyal as ever, Brigham wanted to see Smith's vision realized, but he remained highly skeptical of Missouri as the venue for it. Despite this reservation, Brigham obeyed when Smith announced that he had learned in a revelation that Caldwell County had been the place settled by Adam and Eve after their expulsion from Paradise. The Saints could build their new Zion there, he declared, with the town of Far West as its centerpiece. In obedience to Smith's plan, Brigham secured a piece of land on nearby Mill Creek and set to work energetically building a cabin and putting up fences.

The cabin Brigham built at Mill Creek had to be considerably larger than his home in Kirtland. Not only did he have to shelter his two daughters by his first wife Miriam, but his second wife Mary Ann, after delivering young Joseph Angell Young in 1834, by 1836 had given birth to Brigham Jr. and daughter Mary Ann, named after her mother. The family now comprised seven members. Brigham started building his new homestead eight miles east of Far West, and he also broke the earth and seeded it. All of his skills as farmer and artisan again came into play.

This new home was a very welcome development because Mary Ann needed Brigham's presence, love, and support. During the time that she had stayed behind in Kirtland, she had endured a great deal of harassment on account of the failed bank and Brigham's nighttime flight from his creditors. She had been hard pressed to keep the family afloat in her husband's absence. Such wear and tear on her nervous system had taken its toll, and Brigham was alarmed at her condition when she arrived. He had sent for her and the children as soon as he was able. They traveled by wagon to Wellsville in the eastern part of the state and then took a river steamer west to Richmond. Brigham met them dockside at Richmond and drove them home by wagon to Mill Creek.

As a family man, Brigham was greatly relieved when Smith confided to him that he had had a revelation in which he learned that Brigham's priority until further notice was to regroup and settle his family and see that they were provided for. There would be major assignments for Brigham as an Apostle in the future, but for now his job was to restore his family to a stable existence. He was to retrench. This was a period of general retrenchment for the Saints, as Smith and Rigdon endeavored to shore up the church, so recently shattered by dissension in Kirtland and harassed nearly everywhere by mobs who feared the Mormons' lifestyle and their potential political power as a unified voting bloc. Missouri was rife with warring factions: the abolitionists clashed with the slaveholders, the Native Americans fought with the settlers, settlers belonged to many contentious religious denominations, and now the Mormons were feared statewide for being different and potentially powerful. It was an unsettling time for the Mormons in Missouri—and yet something of a brief respite before even worse threats to the Latter-day Saints.

For roughly the next six months, Brigham concentrated on his family and his farm, putting both on a firm footing. As a result, he did not much participate in meetings and conferences affecting the direction the besieged church would take. Because Brigham stayed mostly on his farm during this time, he did not come in contact with the mobs that once again started to perpetrate violence against the Saints. When a group of Saints attempted to vote in the town of Gallatin in early August, a crowd prevented them and violence resulted.

Then, in September and October, there were other flare-ups of anti-Mormonism within the state. One Mormon settlement was burned to the ground. The violence against Mormons was growing, and at one point Brigham moved his family off the farm and into the town of Far West, eight miles away, for their safety. There, the same issue that had ruined the Kirtland community struck once again: dissension within the church itself. The senior Apostle, Thomas Marsh, suffered a crisis of confidence in Joseph Smith and spoke out against him. Marsh had been put in charge of the printing office in Far West, an important responsibility. Unlike the less senior Apostles, he was to remain at headquarters. Except for Brigham, attending to his family responsibilities, Smith had sent the other Apostles out to preach. Heber Chase Kimball had even been dispatched to spread the Mormon gospel in England, and it was just a few weeks earlier, in late summer, that Heber had returned to Far West and he and Brigham had an emotional reunion.

Now both Brigham and Heber witnessed the spectacle of Thomas Marsh breaking away from the church. After Marsh spoke out against Smith's leadership, he retreated to his printing office and prayed for guidance. When Marsh emerged he spoke to Brigham and Heber, telling them that although God had directed him to believe and support Smith, he could not do it. His main grievance was that Joseph did not accord the Quorum of Twelve proper respect and did not involve them sufficiently in the running of the church. A few short weeks later, Marsh left the church and settled a few miles away. In a surprising development, Orson Hyde followed Marsh and also left the Saints.

But these setbacks were nothing compared to what happened at the end of the month when Governor Lilburn W. Boggs issued his infamous "Exterminating Order" against the Mormons and unleashed the state militia to carry it out. Anti-Mormon feelings had been rising for quite a while. Besieged, Missouri Mormons had organized a band of fighters called the Danites, never officially acknowledged by the church—a mutual protection society, they became the prototype for future Mormon militias. But there was a considerable downside to the creation of the Danites. When they protected the Mormons and their property or when they struck back after Mormons suffered losses of life, limb, or property, these actions only inflamed anti-Mormon sentiment and gave rise to wild rumors of wanton Mormon aggression and violence. Many non-Mormons claimed that the Danites were not merely a defensive force, that they initiated offensive, unprovoked raids against non-Mormons.

Whatever the truth may be, the Danites increased the tension and resulting violence between the Saints and their non-Mormon neighbors.

When the Extermination proclamation was issued, the governor and
other state officials backed the Mormons into a corner and surrounded
them with the Missouri state militia. Then they tricked them. Under a
white flag of truce, Joseph Smith, Sidney Rigdon, and three elders crossed
over the lines and entered the militia camp. Smith sought to negotiate
his people's safety. Instead the five Mormon leaders were arrested and
hauled off to jail. The militia then set upon the Saints, confiscating their
property and, in some cases, sexually assaulting women. Mormon livestock was commandeered or scattered and some buildings were torched.
(Because Heber had recently returned from England and because
Brigham had worked mostly on his farm, neither was on the list of Saints
to be arrested.) General Clark, in command of the Missouri militia, read
out a statement informing the Saints that they were to relinquish their
holdings, gather enough corn for survival, and vacate the state.

Smith, Rigdon, and the other arrested Mormon leaders were taken
to the town of Liberty and placed in jail, chained together in the base-
ment. When Brigham and Heber attempted to visit the imprisoned,
jailers rebuffed them. This left Brigham and Heber—now the two senior
Apostles—no other choice than to convene a council and take command
of the Saints. This they did. Because of the depredations visited upon
the Missouri Saints by the militia and by random mobs, most of the
Saints were destitute—stripped of all means of providing for themselves.
Warned to leave the state or face "extermination," the Saints, without the
means to leave, were desperate for help.

Because the Mormon poor were the responsibility of the presiding
bishop of the local church, Brigham went to see him. His name was
Edward Partridge. Apparently at his wit's end and utterly without means
to help even himself, the bishop told Brigham that the poor would have
to fend for themselves. Such resignation was unacceptable to Brigham.

He immediately set to work to save the community. On January 26, he presided over a general council of the Apostles and elders remaining in the state. Speaking eloquently of the responsibility of those who have means to assist those who have no means, Brigham organized the entire community still possessed of means and induced them to provide the necessary aid to facilitate a general exodus of all Mormons from the state of Missouri. As the leader organizing this exodus, Brigham now had the highest profile of any Saint in the state of Missouri; he had made himself a marked man. He often had to resort to wearing disguises during the day. But by night he roamed and led and counseled.

On February 14, Brigham guided a caravan of wagons east out of Far West, headed for Illinois. From the time he had arrived in Missouri the previous year, Brigham had expected that the Saints would be forced to migrate again, and to the east. And he was right on both counts. Bitter winter conditions assailed the pilgrims in the caravan of wagons bound for Illinois; they had to endure crippling and numbing cold. Yet Brigham kept them moving, and they arrived at the designated gathering place in Illinois, near the Mississippi River, in the first days of spring. While Brigham was leading this wagon train to Illinois, Heber had stayed behind to direct operations in Far West, making sure all the Saints who wanted to leave Missouri were able to. Heber, too, had to hide by day and counsel and lead by night.

Brigham convened a council of the Apostles and elders in Quincy, Illinois, on April 17. He convinced a group of Apostles and elders to return to Far West with him and establish a stone shrine to honor Joseph Smith's revelation that someday a temple would rise on that spot. While a band of senior leaders led by Brigham was doing just that, Joseph Smith and Sidney Ridgon and most of the other imprisoned Saints in Liberty, Missouri, were finally released and started to make their way to Illinois.

A month or so earlier, Brigham and Heber had been able to visit Smith in prison, and he and the other jailed elders had approved

Brigham's actions in organizing and executing the exodus from Missouri. Now Brigham and the band of leaders who had erected the stone shrine in Far West returned to Illinois and had a joyful reunion in early May with Smith and the other elders recently freed from jail. Once again the Saints had met with rejection and scorn in Missouri, but once again this abuse had toughened their resolve. And their exodus from the state of Missouri would provide a template for what would years later be their great triumph—the exodus of the Latter-day Saints from Illinois to the far western deserts beneath the Rockies.

CHAPTER 11

TO BRITAIN

— AND —

BACK

T hough times were difficult for the newly arrived Saints in Illinois in the summer of 1839, there was an impending assignment that the Quorum of Twelve had to undertake no matter the difficulty. This mission had manifested itself to Joseph Smith in a revelation. Knowing that the assignment overhanging the Quorum of Twelve would soon send him wandering afar yet again, Brigham spent the summer trying to secure the position of his family. The Youngs moved upriver from Quincy, Illinois, to temporary lodgings in an abandoned old barracks in Montrose, Iowa, just across the Mississippi River from Nauvoo, Illinois, where many Saints were settling. Mary Ann, pregnant again, was relieved to have a roof over her family's head after their hard journey from Far West and their brief, unsettled stay in the encampment at Quincy.

But because the growing season had coincided with the family's move, Brigham had not been able to sow crops as he would have liked. What made matters worse was an outbreak of malaria that raged through the Mormon community that whole summer. Along the banks of the Mississippi the mosquitoes were always bad, but this especially hot summer they were worse than usual. Many of the Saints fell prey to the disease, including Brigham.

As he lay atremble and sweating profusely from malaria, Brigham contemplated the task that loomed ahead for the Quorum. Smith had bidden them to cross the Atlantic and proselytize in Great Britain. Missionary work had already been started there, but now the Apostles would descend in force and spread the new gospel, seeking converts. Thoughts about the responsibilities lying ahead of him as president of the Quorum, added to his duties as a family man, caused Brigham great concern, and on top of this mental anxiety the malaria took a horrifying toll on his physical strength.

Trusting as ever in God and in the community of Saints, Brigham rose from his sick bed, barely able to walk, and allowed others to help him honor his commitment to the start date set for the Apostles to initiate their journey to England. To compound Brigham's difficulties, his great friend Heber Chase Kimball had also succumbed to malaria. Yet the two men managed to start their trip on time. To do so, Brigham had to be ferried across the Mississippi, then strapped to a horse and guided to Heber's cabin in Nauvoo, Illinois, so weakened was his condition. When Brigham reached the Kimball cabin, he found Heber just as weak.

When word reached Mary Ann of the terrible condition her husband was in after the trip, she, too, crossed the Mississippi and travelled to the Kimball cabin, even though she had given birth only ten days earlier to another daughter, Alice—expanding their family to eight members. Mary Ann, herself weakened by childbirth, nursed Brigham while Heber's wife Vilate nursed him. Despite their weakened condition, both men rose from their sick beds four days later, on September 18, and started east toward the Atlantic coast and, beyond it, England.

Their trip by horse, wagon, and boat progressed slowly, the men staying by night in the homes of Saints along the way. Though Brigham had no way of knowing this, by the time he and Heber reached the house of Brigham's younger brother Lorenzo Dow in Springfield, back in Quincy their father John had died on October 12 at age seventy-six. The character, intelligence, and perseverance that John Young had exhibited all his life would be passed down to later generations through the legacy of Brigham and his other children in the establishment of the Church of Christ of Latter-day Saints. In eulogizing John Young, Joseph Smith described him as a Mormon martyr because of the great toll he had paid during the persecutions and strife suffered in Missouri, where his health had been broken.

Brigham and Heber continued traveling east, though both suffered relapses of the malaria along the way. But they always pushed onward. When they reached Kirtland, they stopped again to visit the former site of so much happiness for the Saints, back before dissension set in. The two Apostles were permitted to preach from the pulpits in the original temple, but when they praised Joseph Smith and chastised the apostates, they roused ire in the elders there. As a consequence, the two would never again be permitted to preach in the original temple, nor would any other members of the church founded by Joseph Smith. Since Brigham and Heber had contributed so much to the building of the Kirtland Temple, their expulsion caused them anguish, even though they realized Kirtland would never again be a key location for the Mormons. Knowing that they had other converts to gather and other temples to build, they quickly moved on.

Brigham and Heber had left Illinois with scarcely any funds, so they had to replenish their money supply by preaching and visiting many fellow Saints along the way. Thus it took six long weeks to finally reach

Manhattan on the last day of January 1840. Brigham and Heber stayed in the house of Parley P. Pratt at 55 Mott Street in lower Manhattan for the next six weeks as they prepared for their journey by visiting the branches of the Mormon church in the city and collecting funds. They toured the city and outfitted themselves with the supplies and gear they would need on the sea passage to Liverpool. After Brigham paid his eighteen-dollar fare and paid in one more dollar as his share for the cook's services, he left for England with fifty cents to his name on March 29, 1840, accompanied by Heber, Parley Pratt and his brother Orson, George A. Smith, and Reuben Hedlock. The five missionaries boarded the *Patrick Henry*, a packet ship operated by the Black Ball Line.

The ship was not long underway before Brigham fell violently seasick, the result no doubt of his still weakened condition from his recent bout with malaria. He had lost far too much weight, and he became lightheaded and acutely sick to his stomach onboard the ship. His steerage quarters were also spartan and scarcely ventilated; the air there was fetid and sour. Being in the bow of the ship, Brigham's quarters bore the brunt of the rough seas, bobbing and pitching wildly when, eight days out of port, the *Patrick Henry* encountered a heavy storm that damaged the bulwarks of the ship. As a result, water poured down the deck hatches and flooded the lower compartments, including Brigham's steerage quarters in the bow. Brigham endured all of this discomfort while sick and prostrate in his bunk. An injury from a few weeks earlier also contributed to his discomfort. While waiting to board a Brooklyn ferry, Brigham had tripped and taken a hard fall dockside, dislocating his shoulder.

Under these conditions, Brigham had scarcely any appetite—not that the meager ship's fare would have done him much good. When the *Patrick Henry* docked in Liverpool on April 6, his clothes hung on him. Between malaria and seasickness, he was emaciated. Waiting on the wharf for the five Apostles was Willard Richards, who had accomplished so much already in spreading the word of *The Book of Mormon* in England. When Brigham disembarked, he was so battered by sustained illness that Richards did not at first recognize him.

But Brigham's marvelous recuperative powers soon had him back in the swing of things, meeting his obligations as an Apostle. This journey marked his first trip on foreign soil, except for the excellent missionary work he had accomplished in Canada. Heber had travelled to England three years earlier to establish a Mormon presence there, but Brigham was experiencing it for the first time. On Heber's previous trip, he had made Preston the center of his outreach. Brigham naturally followed his friend's lead and set up an operations center in Preston from which the Apostles could move outward in their quest for converts.

On the earlier 1837 mission to England, Heber and the other elders accompanying him had baptized the first nine English converts outdoors in the Ripple River in sight of a large crowd. The baptisms had a deep impact, and the Mormons were being noticed in England. At this time the Industrial Revolution was in full, brutal force and the English working class was treated abysmally, kept in horrifying poverty, and disenfranchised. The Mormon promise of gathering in the American Zion and bettering oneself in all aspects of life made a positive impression on many converts.

Within two weeks, an eighth Apostle was added to the seven Apostles gathered in England when Brigham ordained Willard Richards. Brigham brought his vast aptitude for effective organization into play on this English mission. Fellow Apostle Orson Hyde and elders Willard Richards and Joseph Fielding had accompanied Heber on his previous trip to England. These four had proselytized effectively and established a strong Mormon organization. Joseph Fielding and Willard Richards had stayed behind in Preston when the other two returned to America in 1838. Brigham now convened a council of the Apostles in England and laid out an agenda. This council is often called "the first Council of the Twelve among the Nations."

And then Brigham wasted no time in calling together a general council of all the Saints then in England. It drew sixteen hundred attendees. Two well-off converts donated three hundred and fifty pounds and Brigham used it for publicity, applying the public relations lessons he had learned from Joseph Smith. A printing press was established and a new publication launched, titled the *Latter-day Saints Millennial Star*. Parley Pratt, a seasoned writer, served as the editor of this bimonthly periodical. The first issue appeared in late May 1840 in Manchester, within seven weeks of Brigham's landing at Liverpool. With the donated money Brigham also ordered the first printing in England of *The Book of Mormon* and of a Mormon hymnbook. The importance of emigration and the need to gather in the new Zion in America was given enormous emphasis from all the Mormon preachers.

In the space of two months, Brigham organized the first group of converts to emigrate to America. Although this initial group consisted of only forty people, it provided the prototype for the larger emigration that followed rapidly. This first group left in June of 1840 on the packet ship *Britannia* and sailed around the Florida peninsula and into the port of New Orleans. From there, the trip up the Mississippi to Nauvoo by steamboat was comparatively easy. Very soon thereafter, larger contingents of converts shipped for America, their passage organized and overseen by Brigham with assistance from John Taylor and Willard Richards. The Mormons had the collective knowledge and business acumen to handle all details of emigrant sailings to America, thereby protecting largely uneducated and underprivileged converts from being cheated by shipping agents. One such ship of Mormon emigrants to America drew the interest of a young English journalist named Charles Dickens, who wrote a lively article about it full of piquant details.

While in England, Brigham convened a total of four general conferences. The last occurred on April 2, 1841, exactly one year after Brigham had landed in Liverpool. It convened in Manchester, where the Apostles founded a strong branch. Astonishingly, there were nearly six and a half thousand attendees. No further proof is needed of the Apostles' hard work or of the enthusiasm with which the English took to the new church and its doctrine. In fact, by then Brigham had organized matters so well that branches of the Mormon church had sprouted in Scotland, Wales, and Ireland. Heber Chase Kimball, aided by elders Wilford Woodruff and John Taylor, had also managed to establish a strong Mormon presence in London.

So effective were Brigham and his colleagues at spreading the word that traditional British clerics became upset and began to complain about the Latter-day Saints. Their verbal assault on the Mormons was nothing new, of course. Back home in Illinois—and in New York, Ohio, and Missouri—the Saints had suffered from similar resentments. When he was in England, Brigham had concerns about how those resentments might be affecting his family back home. And in Britain there was the familiar skepticism about the validity of Mormon doctrine—in addition to social and political concerns aroused by the sympathy to the poor and underprivileged openly exhibited by the Saints, and by their assurances that vastly better living conditions, political freedoms, and educational and employment opportunities awaited converts in America.

These assurances were emphatically true. And they made Mormonism very attractive to the British working class. During their stay, the Apostles managed to baptize between seven and eight thousand converts, to print five thousand copies of *The Book of Mormon*, to distribute three thousand copies of the hymnbook, and to disseminate fifty thousand tracts. They also helped a thousand converts emigrate to America. In addition, the Apostles left behind in England a functioning shipping agency run entirely by Mormons, to make the journey to America for future converts wishing to emigrate to the new Zion possible.

With their mission accomplished, Brigham and his fellow missionaries sailed for home from Liverpool on the *Rochester* on April 20, 1841.

Brigham and Mary Ann's home in Nauvoo, Illinois. *Library of Congress*

With him were fellow Apostles Heber C. Kimball, Orson Pratt, John Taylor, Willard Richards, George A. Smith, and Wilford Woodruff. Apostle Parley Pratt stayed behind to head up the British Mission and to edit and publish the *Latter-day Saints Millennial Star*. Apostle Orson Hyde remained behind to prepare for his mission to the Holy Land as directed by Joseph Smith. The Apostles encountered some rough seas in their month-long passage back across the Atlantic, but Brigham, no longer weakened by malaria or hampered by his injured shoulder, fared better than he had on the way over. After the *Rochester* pulled into New York Harbor, Brigham and his companions stayed in the area for six weeks, overseeing branches of the Mormon church and engaging in a round of vigorous preaching.

Then Brigham and his fellow Apostles travelled down to Philadelphia by steamer and from there took canal boats and trains to Pittsburgh. From Pittsburgh they sailed down the Ohio River to the Mississippi and there boarded a riverboat for the trip up to Nauvoo. Arriving home on

July 1, the Apostles were met by a cheering crowd of Saints on the landing headed by Joseph Smith. Among them Brigham spotted Mary Ann and his older children. When Brigham joined his family, he learned to his delight that they had a new home in Nauvoo, a small cabin that was a big improvement over the improvised apartment in the abandoned barracks across the river in Montrose, Iowa.

CHAPTER 12

INCREASED
• — • — •
RESPONSIBILITIES

B y the time Brigham returned to Nauvoo, he had been gone nearly two years. His oldest daughter Elizabeth was sixteen and of marriageable age, according to the custom of that era, and his newest daughter, Alice, had gone from a newborn when Brigham left for England in September of 1839 to a full-fledged toddler. During his absence, Mary Ann had once again shown her mettle by shouldering all domestic responsibilities, even managing the move across the river from Montrose into the new family home, the newly built cabin in Nauvoo, not far from the center of the booming town where Joseph Smith had his new residence, called "the Homestead." He and his family were domiciled there while on the same site a newer and better family house for them, called "the Mansion House," was being built. Brigham's new home was very near all the new homes of the Apostles and elders of the church.

The Saints were now engaged in building what at the time was the second-largest city in the entire state. Within two years Nauvoo, situated in Hancock County, would have a population of nearly twelve thousand residents, just shy of Chicago's population at that time; this exponential growth in population was the result of Mormons "gathering" there.

While Brigham and the other Apostles had been abroad making converts, Smith had labored feverishly in Illinois to obtain a charter for the city of Nauvoo unlike any other ever granted. The Illinois legislature had agreed to grant Nauvoo wide powers and nearly full autonomy. The city could have its own nearly autonomous administration; its own court system, including the right to issue writs of habeas corpus; its own militia, called the Nauvoo Legion; and its own university. Under this uniquely powerful charter, Smith planned to embellish the city with the greatest temple yet constructed by the Mormons. It was to dominate the cityscape, standing out prominently on the apex of a hill rising above the river flats. In addition, a modern hotel with all the amenities would rise near the riverbanks to accommodate the projected influx of converts and immigrants.

Excitement ran high among the Saints about Nauvoo's potential as a permanent headquarters for their new church, but Brigham remembered the horrible treatment previously accorded the Mormons in New York, in Ohio, and especially in Missouri. Sensitive as ever, he detected undercurrents in Illinois of the resentments that seemed to stalk the Saints no matter where they went or how exemplary their behavior was.

The new cabin in Nauvoo was on land so marshy it could not be worked properly until Brigham managed to drain it. But once drained it proved spectacularly suited to farming, and Brigham set about planting the crops to feed his large family. It pleased Brigham that within days of his arrival back in Nauvoo, Joseph Smith visited him to relate another revelation. Brigham was no longer to sacrifice his family to his duties as a missionary. His vagabonding days as a preacher of the new gospel were over. He was to devote himself to being a family man and a provider—God had instructed Joseph Smith to convey this message to him. Both Brigham and Mary Ann rejoiced at this news, though neither had ever complained of the hardships attached to Brigham's proselytizing duties as an Apostle and head of the Quorum.

Brigham soon received welcome news about the Quorum as well. A month after arriving home, he learned from Joseph Smith that the Quorum of Twelve would have expanded responsibilities. No longer would the Apostles concentrate their efforts principally on proselytizing. From this point forward they would also assume a large role in the administration of the church's affairs. Up until now, the First Presidency had directed the administrative affairs with help from the stake presidents, from the members called to the high councils, and from the bishops. Up until now, these leaders had not been subject to the authority of the Twelve, but going forward they would be.

When Joseph Smith was unable to attend an August 16 meeting because of the death of his infant son, Don Carlos, he announced that Brigham would preside over the meeting in his stead. As president of the Twelve Apostles, Brigham was now second in command of the church, after Joseph Smith. In the notes of this meeting, Brigham is humble in his assumption of power and nowhere seems to be overreaching his subsidiary role. Yet he assumes the leadership Smith clearly intended him to take. Brigham stated clearly at this meeting that, as always, he would be obedient to directives originating with God as channeled through Joseph Smith.

The simple reality was that Smith had seen the magnificent work accomplished by the Apostles in Great Britain under Brigham's stewardship. Foreign converts were streaming into Nauvoo, just as native converts were also pouring in from New England and New York, and especially from Ohio and Missouri, fleeing persecution or dissension in the Saints' ranks.

In making these administrative changes, Smith was acknowledging the managerial potential of the Twelve, based on the Apostles' astounding success in the British Isles. He was also rewarding Brigham's superior leadership and administrative skills, which he had spotted all the way back in Kirtland when he first met Brigham on that fateful autumn day in 1832. Nine years later, Smith believed that Brigham had learned enough from him about running the church to assume the tactical role of chief executive officer, in support of Smith's strategic role as chairman of the board. Smith would plan, Brigham would implement. Smith would order, Brigham would execute. Smith realized that his strength resided in the spiritual realm, as a visionary, while Brigham, though deeply religious, was a more gifted executive, a master organizer, and an energetic doer blessed with preternatural common sense and enormous practical know-how.

Following Brigham's lead, the eleven other Apostles in the Quorum stepped up to the challenge Joseph Smith had issued and began, like Brigham, to take charge of church affairs as equals to the members of the First Presidency. Just as Joseph had groomed and schooled Brigham, so too, in combination with Joseph, Brigham now groomed and schooled the other Apostles for the larger responsibilities that would now fall to them. During the following ten months, Smith convened many meetings and seminars with the Twelve. At these seminars he would preach and elucidate church beliefs and principles, instructing the Twelve on such matters as the importance of charity and the centrality of *The Book of Mormon*. He underscored the importance of faith and the essential spirituality that imbued the church from top to bottom. In effect, he conducted an intensified, fast-track seminary.

The key new doctrine Smith introduced at this time, in the summer of 1841, was "plural marriage," as the Saints prefer to call it—more commonly known as polygamy. Since 1831, when he found evidence for it in the Old Testament, Joseph Smith had been convinced that the Bible

validated this practice. At that time he had been studying the Bible vigorously with Oliver Cowdery and realized that some Old Testament
patriarchs had more than one wife. The practice had also been approved
in revelations to Joseph Smith himself, in *The Book of Mormon* Jacob,
2-27-30. Smith held that it was imperative for his new Christian church
to embrace all ancient biblical principles, and therefore plural marriage
needed to be included.

Because of its inhumane aspects—particularly its potential for harm
to both women and children—polygamy is generally held in low regard.
It was certainly frowned on in mid-nineteenth-century America, when
Joseph Smith introduced it and justified the new dogma by saying that
it was based on Scripture. The vast majority of American Christians at
the time did not accept this interpretation of the Bible, and the practice
of polygamy further alienated mainstream Americans from Mormonism. The practice also caused controversy, dissension, and schism within
the church for years to come, with several branches of Mormonism
breaking away and forming their own new religions.

Brigham and most of the other Apostles were at first thrown by this
revelation, fearing polygamy's potential to inspire even more abuse of
the Mormon community by outsiders. Yet, after counseling from Smith,
they came to accept the new doctrine and to embrace the new practice—
at least in the short run. But plural marriage would eventually spark
trouble, causing a new round of dissension among some elders and
believers. Smith's motives were doubted by some of his followers—as
they have been over the years by some of his biographers. So, too, were
his methods. Back then women had fewer rights than they have today.
Critics accuse Smith of acting out of a raging ego and rampant libido,
coercing women—usually very young women—into having sex with
him by convincing them that their earthy security and their heavenly
reward would both be forfeited if they did not.

The resistance to the practice of polygamy by some elders and other Saints ultimately provoked a rift in 1843 that proved insuperable. Dissenters to the dogma of plural marriage considered that what Smith was doing amounted to statutory rape (a charge sustained down to the present day by his detractors and critics—by radical feminists but also by mainstream champions of human rights). Several members of the church became so heated in their opposition that they formed a coalition of dissenters and went after Smith in an alleged assassination plot, concocted under the leadership of dissidents William Law and his business partner Robert D. Foster.

These dissidents eventually purchased a press and launched a publication titled the *Nauvoo Expositor*, whose sole purpose was to counter the official Mormon publications Smith had set up in Nauvoo. From the very beginning of his church, Smith, clearly a promotional and public relations genius before his time, had set up presses in each successive headquarters to spread the word of his new gospel. Nauvoo was no exception. The official Latter-day Saints' newspaper at this time was called the *Nauvoo Neighbor*, and the monthly magazine went by the title *Times and Seasons*. Smith also issued a Nauvoo edition of *The Book of Mormon* and numerous tracts and pamphlets on doctrine and church history, as was his practice in all previous church headquarters.

These publications had been placed under the supervision of the Twelve as part of the delegation of administrative power in the fall of 1841. For the next two years, Brigham and his fellow Apostles had capably overseen these official church publications. In those same two years, Brigham had spent most of his time on administrative duties in Nauvoo except for short proselytizing trips back east to visit and inspire local church branches there and to gather more converts.

In addition, Brigham had suffered a near fatal bout of what is believed today to have been scarlet fever. He may also have suffered from another unidentified infectious disease simultaneously. His condition worsened to the point where he was unable to breathe. Mary Ann alertly saved his life by applying what today we call mouth-to-mouth resuscitation.

Upon his recovery, Brigham was able to begin building a substantial brick house for Mary Ann and his family, his two daughters with Miriam and his four surviving children with Mary Ann. This new brick house, like the cabin, was not far from the home of another wife Brigham had married—"celestially," as the Saints said—after considerable soul searching. The Mormons also used the term "sealing" to describe such unions. Brigham's first plural wife was Lucy Ann Decker Seeley, legally married to Dr. Isaac Seeley when Brigham spotted her and lured her away from her husband. Brigham married her with Mary Ann's consent and blessing on June 15, 1842, in a ceremony presided over by Joseph Smith.

In the spring of 1844, slightly less than two years after marrying Lucy Ann Decker Seeley, Brigham married her sister Clarissa, two months shy of her sixteenth birthday. Setting a brisk pace, in under two years' time Brigham acquired four celestial brides.

With Lucy, his first "celestial" bride, twenty on their wedding day, Brigham would eventually have seven children. After her marriage to Brigham, Lucy continued to live in the house her first husband had provided for her in Nauvoo, and there she raised her children by Brigham until they all moved to Utah in the late 1840s as part of the great exodus west. Lucy and Brigham's first child, son Brigham Heber, born on June 19, 1845, in Nauvoo, is considered the first child of Mormon polygamy. Faithful, intelligent, devout, and devoted, Lucy stayed by Brigham for the rest of his life and outlived him by thirteen years.

Less than three months after Brigham married Lucy, on August 1, 1842, Mary Ann delivered her and Brigham's fifth child and third daughter, Luna. That autumn Mary Ann attended two more sealings of young women to Brigham, lending her approval and support. She had been convinced by her husband that such actions were in concert with God's plans for them and for the good of the church, of the kingdom on earth. Unlike Joseph Smith, Brigham was open and direct with his wife about the practice of celestial marriage. Smith had conducted most of his early sealings in the room above his store, in secret, and totally unbeknownst to his wife Emma.

This deception was wise because Emma detested this new practice and despised her husband for introducing it into the church as new doctrine. From the very first she heard about it, the practice of polygamy distressed Emma Smith and strained her marriage to Joseph. Thus her husband was stealthy about his sealings and kept them from his wife. Not so Brigham: he told Mary Ann about celestial marriage and about its alleged sacred origins in Scripture as revealed to Joseph Smith. Joseph Smith was not the only object of Emma's wrath. She never forgave Brigham, as the second most powerful leader in the church, for putting his stamp of approval on what she considered her husband's flimsy justification for his licentiousness. After Smith's death, Emma broke with Brigham irrevocably over polygamy, spoiling his intentions to seal her as he had done with several of Smith's celestial brides. Emma knew her mind and married a Gentile—the Mormon term for non-Mormons—Major Lewis Bidamon, in 1847 in a Methodist Episcopal church, three years after Smith's death.

In contrast, after eight years of blissful solo marriage to Brigham, Mary Ann would go on to endure, stoically and quietly, his fifty-four additional wives and his fifty additional children. She loved the six children she had with Brigham, and he always treated her and the children well. Later in Utah, Mary Ann would encounter resentment from many of Brigham's younger wives because they believed Brigham accorded her priority treatment. She lived with her children in Salt Lake City in what was called the "White House," spacious quarters compared with the crowded conditions endured by most of the other wives and their children living in the cramped Beehive House or the Lion House. But

Mary Ann had paid her dues. Years later in Salt Lake City, the other wives would refer to Mary Ann, sometimes derisively, as "Mother Young" and "the Queen." She bore many indignities as Brigham's wife and apparently endured this lifestyle out of her love for her husband, her sense of duty, and her religious convictions. After her death, however, a friend of hers asserted in a eulogy that Mary Ann was a sensitive woman and her unorthodox marriage and unconventional lifestyle had caused her much suffering. Given human nature, it is hard to conceive how it could have been otherwise.

1843 saw another big change for Brigham. A little over a year after Brigham married Lucy—a year that Brigham spent building Mary Ann's new brick house and also working to build up his commercial interests in Nauvoo, mostly in real estate and in construction—Brigham, at Smith's request, traveled back east on a tour to preach and raise funds among the Saints for the building of the Nauvoo Temple and the Nauvoo House, the planned hotel along the riverbanks. On July 7, 1843, accompanied by Wilford Woodruff and E. P. Maginn, Brigham boarded the steamer *Rapids* and headed downriver to St. Louis. From there the three fundraisers traveled by coach and by boat in an easterly direction, stopping at Louisville, Pittsburgh, and Philadelphia.

At each stop, they preached and also raised contributions from the Saints belonging to established local branches of the church. Brigham, now in his seventh year as an Apostle, displayed his usual passion in carrying out this assignment from Smith, despite earlier assurances that he would never again have to leave his family behind and make long journeys away from them. On this trip, Brigham was distressed to learn in correspondence from Mary Ann that the family had been hit with a severe illness. All the children except young Joseph came down with scarlet fever. Tragically, shortly after Mary Ann wrote to inform Brigham that this plague had passed and all had survived, their daughter Mary Ann, her mother's namesake, fell ill and died from what was described as "dropsy." Little Mary Ann was coming up on her seventh birthday when she succumbed. Because in those days the primitive mail service was erratic and because Brigham was traveling, preaching, and fundraising at a rapid and unpredictable pace, he did not learn of his daughter's demise until she had long since been buried, her mother having handled all the funeral details by the time Brigham and his companions returned to Nauvoo three months later on October 22.

All the while Brigham was away, word of the new doctrine of plural marriage was continuing to seep out of the clannish Mormon community in Nauvoo. The dissenters among the faithful were conducting a whisper campaign fueled by their disapproval, and the news that Mormons were practicing polygamy riled the anti-Mormon agitators in Illinois.

In seeking to render his church and its latest headquarters community safe and secure, Joseph Smith had become heavily involved in state and local politics in Illinois, just as he had in Ohio and in Missouri. That is how he obtained the unique city charter for Nauvoo, granting the growing Mormon community such broad powers of autonomy. A young politician in the Illinois House of Representatives named Abraham Lincoln, a tolerant and understanding man, had helped the Mormons obtain this uniquely powerful city charter. (Later, as president, Lincoln would pursue the same tolerant and benevolent policy toward the Mormons—though by then Brigham detested Lincoln, as he detested all politicians, especially those most powerful ones back in Washington, D.C.)

Yet, as Brigham had feared it would, the same pattern of resentment by the local non-Mormons was asserting itself again in Illinois. The anti-Mormon hostility simmered just below the surface. With word of plural marriage spreading wider, this growing resentment steadily intensified. Following the familiar pattern first established years earlier in New York, and seen again in Ohio and in Missouri, many non-Mormons in

Illinois were disturbed by the increasing Mormon political power; Mormons were now a sizable voting bloc in the state. They were also incredibly active in the state capital, endeavoring through their lobbyists to attain the political goals they sought to achieve.

In the fall of 1843, fierce opposition to the Saints erupted in two communities near Nauvoo—Warsaw and Carthage, the Hancock County seat. Violence flared up and some Mormon property was damaged. The political climate had deteriorated so badly for the Mormons that, in the last months of 1843, they polled the leading candidates for president in the election scheduled for the following autumn of 1844, asking the candidates to take a stand on the Mormons' situation. The Saints wanted to know if reparations would be made for the damages they had already suffered, and also whether the federal government would protect their property and their lives going forward. The results were discouraging in the extreme. Only two of the several candidates, Henry Clay and John C. Calhoun, bothered to reply. Worse, neither reply held out any real hope for permanent security for the Mormons.

As a result, in January of 1844, Joseph Smith received approval from the church hierarchy to pursue his plans to run for president. This may well have been an ill-advised step, an instance of overreaching ambition. Besides the incendiary effect of learning that the Mormons practiced polygamy, without doubt the catalyzing incident that inflamed hostility to the Mormons in Illinois was Joseph Smith's announcement that he would stand as a candidate for president. Non-Mormons simply did not want a Mormon leader and a polygamist occupying the highest office in the land.

CHAPTER 13

THE ASSASSINATION

After several high councils convened for the purpose of strategizing Joseph Smith's run for president, Brigham Young effectively became Smith's campaign manager. The church authorities had decided to use "all honorable means" to bring Smith to victory. Quite obviously, the Mormon elders had decided to circumvent local and national authorities and take their case directly to the people. As president of the Quorum of Twelve, Brigham appointed speakers and preachers and assigned them territories to canvass. To this purpose he convened a general conference in April at which 344 brethren committed themselves to go on the campaign trail to promote Smith's candidacy.

Applying his formidable organizational skills, Brigham mapped out a detailed plan calling for the 344 speakers to fan out across the then twenty-six states and conduct what Brigham called forty-seven "general conferences" between the beginning of May and the middle of September.

The election of 1844 would be the last presidential election held on different dates in different states; by the middle of September, the campaign season would be over. The final general conference was to begin in Washington, D.C., on September 7 and conclude eight days later. Brigham and Smith figured that this final conference would garner huge amounts of publicity and sweep Smith into office.

Smith ran as the elected mayor of Nauvoo and a political independent. His platform was simple: he proposed the redemption of slaves by selling public lands and by reducing the size of Congress and slashing congressional salaries; the annexation of Texas, Oregon, and parts of Canada; the stabilization of international rights on the high seas; the closure of all prisons; the promotion of free market capitalism; and the re-establishment of the National Bank that had been abolished by Andrew Jackson a dozen years earlier, in 1832. Brimming with enthusiasm, Brigham directed the campaigners on just how they were to present Smith's platform. Besides spelling out the political agenda Smith proposed, the Mormon orators were not to neglect their ecclesiastical obligations. They were to preach the Gospel in all its simple glory and to remain humble and meek while doing so.

In training the campaigners, Brigham also made good use of a political tract Smith had published, using his self-declared rank of general in the Nauvoo Legion, the Mormon militia. Titled *General Smith's Views of the Powers and Policy of the Government of the United States*, this tract purported to take a balanced position on the platforms of the two leading candidates of the established parties: Whig nominee Henry Clay and Democratic frontrunner Martin Van Buren. The tract was a bit disingenuous in its feigned balance; Smith had expressed low opinions of both Clay and Van Buren in the past.

In his excellent biography, *Brigham Young: Pioneer Prophet*, John G. Turner reports that Smith characterized Clay as a "black-leg in politics" and called Van Buren "a fop or a fool." Brigham encouraged the campaigners to read this tract aloud to gathered Mormons as they mixed their political message with the Gospel—a mixture that would seem to be at odds with the American Constitution's separation of church and state. But like Smith, Brigham didn't care much for this separation. Smith had lately begun to refer to all of America as the new Zion, thus erasing any distinction between political and religious matters. This Mormon attitude did not sit well with non-Mormon Americans who did not wish to see democracy replaced with a theocracy, or, as Smith called it, a "theodemocracy."

With a firm handclasp, Brigham, travelling with fellow Apostles Heber Kimball and Lyman Wight, took leave of candidate Smith on the wharf before the steamer *Osprey* pushed off and steamed downriver to St. Louis. As the three men wound their way to Pittsburgh, Brigham would have time onboard steamers to plan further details and objectives for Smith's campaign. At Pittsburgh, Kimball and Wight pushed on toward Washington, D.C., to prepare for the big concluding general conference planned there over the course of eight days from September 7 through 15. Meanwhile, Brigham met John C. Page in Pittsburgh, and the two started campaigning in that area together, always mixing Smith's political agenda with the basic tenets of Mormonism. Brigham, like all the traveling campaigners, had only a vague idea what was brewing back in Nauvoo, where the situation for the Saints and for Smith was rapidly worsening. As Smith's presidential campaign had geared up under Brigham's capable management, things were going awry in Illinois. Even as Brigham had boarded the steamer *Osprey* for his campaigning swing back through the East, all was not well in Nauvoo.

There was dissension within the ranks of the Saints. William Law was the chief builder and developer in Nauvoo, and he stood to make a fortune there if the Mormons were not driven out. Law, whom Smith had made one of his chief advisors in the Office of the Presidency, had immediately broken with him over the doctrine of polygamy when word of it leaked out two years earlier. Law rightly feared and predicted that the doctrine of polygamy would bring scorn and violence down upon the Saints. By this time, Law and his business partner had joined several other dissidents wishing to rid the Saints of Smith's leadership.

Already for years there had been attempts to have Smith extradited to Missouri to stand trial for alleged crimes associated with the Saints during their troubled tenure there. These extradition attempts had always been thwarted in the Nauvoo courts, which Smith controlled as mayor and theocrat. It had been alleged that Smith and his bodyguard Porter Rockwell masterminded an assassination attempt in May of 1842 against Lilburn W. Boggs, the Missouri governor who four years earlier had spearheaded the campaign to "exterminate" the Mormons in his state. At this time, the Mormons were facing an increased outcry that they were seeking political domination, that they had engineered a murder plot toward this end, and that immoral practices were running rampant within their communities.

The presence of the Nauvoo Legion—the Mormon militia—did not have a calming effect on the non-Mormons alarmed by the Saints and pushing to expel them from Illinois. Back in Missouri, many anti-Mormons were still smarting from the activities, just a few years earlier, of the never officially recognized Danites, the prototype Mormon militia that had acted in a vigilante capacity in that state. The Danites had organized in self-defense in response to the anti-Mormon violence, but the fact that the Mormons had fought back and even gone on the offensive only exacerbated the mob violence. Now Law and his fellow Mormon dissidents who had broken with Smith over polygamy sought to aid Smith's enemies in Missouri and have him transported there to stand trial on various charges.

At this time, Brigham was mostly campaigning, preaching, and mixing the two in Massachusetts. He mistook the unsettling news from Nauvoo about the opposition to Smith for just the usual Mormon-bashing.

Brigham was well aware of violent attacks on Mormons—violence had just broken out at his own evening speaking engagement at the Melodeon Theatre in downtown Boston on July 1. But he underestimated the real danger to Smith. Apparently, unlike Brigham, Smith had inklings of his impending doom. He started to preach and counsel with a nearly hysterical fervor about what to do should he not be able to continue to lead the church. Smith proved to be prescient about this matter, as he had been about so many others.

William Law and his business partner Robert Foster had imported a rival printing press to Nauvoo on May 7. They set to work to commence countering the official Mormon publications with the launch of the *Nauvoo Expositor*. As it turned out, they needed only a month to achieve publication. The sole aim of the *Expositor* was to denounce Smith and remove him from power in the church and the city government. Editorial attacks against Smith and the Saints had already been launched by Thomas Sharp, the publisher of the *Warsaw Signal*, the newspaper in the town nearest to Nauvoo. Sharp had railed against Smith as "a dangerous man" for years. And John C. Bennett, a Mormon convert who had risen high in Nauvoo before Smith disciplined and excommunicated him for sexual misconduct, had aided Sharp in his campaign against Smith by publishing a book in 1842 titled *The History of the Saints; or, An Exposé of Joe Smith and Mormonism*. The book sold well and garnered national attention in magazines and newspapers.

Shortly after the June 7 publication of the inaugural edition of the *Nauvoo Expositor*, Smith's defenders stormed the dissidents' new press and destroyed it—following its denunciation by Smith and a high council of Mormon elders. The consequences of this rash action were disastrous for the Mormons. Smashing a printing press and silencing the *Expositor* violated freedom of the press, a basic American right. Quite rightly, a hue and cry went up denouncing the Saints. Smith and the members of the high council faced charges of inciting a riot. By order of Illinois Governor Thomas Ford, Smith and his fellow defendants were subject to the jurisdiction of the courts in Carthage, the county seat, rather than to the jurisdiction of the Nauvoo courts controlled by Smith under the powerful city charter granted the Mormons years earlier by the Illinois state legislature. That charter, masterfully lobbied for and fashioned by Smith himself, had in the past allowed Smith impunity. But this time the state authorities immediately arrested Smith and placed him in the Carthage jail, along with his brother Hyrum.

Smith's arrest precipitated the darkest moment in the history of the Church of the Latter-day Saints. On the evening of June 27, 1844, despite personal guarantees of their safety from Governor Ford, Joseph Smith and his brother Hyrum were shot in their cells at the Carthage jail. An enraged mob with blackened faces, brandishing weapons and led by militiamen from Warsaw and Carthage, laid siege to the building at about 5:00 p.m. local time. After storming up the stairs from the ground floor, they shot the inmates where they stood. Joseph Smith, his body pierced by bullets, staggered to a second story window and fell from it to land on the ground below. His final words were a gurgled attempt to voice an exhortation for heavenly help: "O Lord my God." In the mayhem, the militiamen also injured the Mormon Apostle John Taylor who, along with Brigham's cousin Willard Richards, was visiting Joseph and Hyrum at the time.

Trial by jury, rather than mob violence, would have been the civilized and sane way to rein in Joseph Smith's megalomania. But Smith's own ill-considered actions in inciting a riot that ended in the smashing of a printing press did precipitate his own doom.

With the demise of Joseph Smith, the fate of the Church of Jesus Christ of Latter-day Saints altered forever. As could be expected, Smith left a huge power vacuum. Into that vacuum stepped Brigham Young.

CHAPTER 14

THE NEW
· · ·
LEADER

Because the mail system in 1844 was so primitive and slow, Brigham did not learn of the assassination of Joseph Smith for weeks. For about a month he had been campaigning in New England, using Boston as a base and spiraling out from there to barnstorm in the surrounding towns. He was stumping hard for Joseph Smith's presidential candidacy under the banner of what Smith had dubbed the Jeffersonian Democratic Party.

By early July, rumors had started to swirl about what had happened back in Nauvoo and in the Carthage jail. On July 9, when Brigham and Orson Pratt were speaking in Salem, they first heard an unsubstantiated rumor about the assassination, but they had no definite proof of what had transpired. Vilate, Brigham's now-fourteen-year-old daughter by first wife Miriam, was staying with relatives in Salem, and Brigham's happiness in being with her was disturbed but not shattered by the rumor about Smith. There had been many wild rumors before about Joseph Smith and about the Mormons in general.

So Brigham and Orson Pratt calmly moved on to Petersboro, their next scheduled campaign stop. A large conference had been called there, and Brigham looked forward to enlisting many voters on Smith's behalf. But a week later, while still at the Petersboro conference, Brigham learned in a letter from fellow Apostle Wilford Woodruff the grim and devastating details of the twin murders of Joseph and Hyrum Smith. Brigham was devastated, but to his credit he did not fall apart, even though he knew for certain now that the dual murders had indeed taken place two weeks earlier. Brigham was always strong and controlled in public. Other Mormons wept openly upon hearing the horrible news—including Woodruff, when Brigham met him a day later in Boston. But Brigham did not indulge his grief publicly on hearing the news, though his journal attests to how upset and grief-stricken he was.

Instead Brigham remained impassive and steadfast in the public eye. He had followed Smith for a dozen years and embraced him as a true prophet of God. Under Smith, Brigham had been ordained and had learned, by testament and by example, how to organize and lead people. In the last few years, Smith had granted Brigham the powers of the "Second Anointing." This special ritual had endowed Brigham with the highest priestly powers attainable by a Mormon. It is more than possible— indeed, it is likely—that Brigham intuited instantly upon learning of Smith's demise that for years Smith had groomed him for the ultimate church leadership role now looming before him. With his keen powers of discernment, Brigham doubtless knew that great responsibilities lay before him and that now was the time to think and not to emote.

Brigham and Smith had much in common, including their ability to intuit events. Ample evidence exists that Smith sensed his impending death. His determined preaching in his last months indicates this, as does his special attention in grooming Brigham for the larger role Smith sensed that Brigham would play in the continuance of his new church. Then again, Smith's reckless actions in causing a riot and inciting the destruction of a printing press were so starkly provocative that it can be argued he courted his own death.

Brigham would later recollect that on the evening of June 27, while the murders were taking place in Carthage, he was sitting in the Boston train station with Woodruff waiting to go to Salem and visit daughter Vilate. This prospect pleased him, yet, as he later wrote, he suddenly felt a "heavy depression" he could not explain. So severe was it that he had difficulty conversing with Woodruff while waiting for the train. He wrote that he could not assign any reasons for "my peculiar feelings."

On July 16, a week after receiving the confirming letter in Petersboro, Brigham finally succumbed to his overwhelming grief at the loss of Smith. Brigham vented his grief at the Boston home of a devout Saint named Sister Vose. Brigham and many of the Apostles had gathered there to plan what they should next do. They had been scattered throughout New England speaking for Smith's presidential campaign, now a moot point. Among them in the privacy of the Vose residence, Brigham broke down and wept openly. No doubt giving in to his melancholy was healthy for Brigham and for the other Apostles present. They needed to expunge their sorrow so they could think more clearly. The larger and weightier question of what actions to take next loomed over them.

Grieving along with Brigham were his best friend Heber Chase Kimball and also Orson Pratt, Wilford Woodruff, and Orson Hyde—all fellow Apostles. Lyman Wight, another Apostle, joined them a week later, having traveled from a distant campaigning location. Now half of the Quorum of Twelve Apostles was present and able to plan what must be done in the best interests of the church. And here again, Brigham's remarkable talents played a major role.

Upon first reading the letter confirming the murders, while still in Petersboro, Brigham had said that his immediate concern was whether

Smith had taken the keys to the kingdom with him into the celestial realm. That issue was now about to be resolved. Sitting next to Brigham at the meeting at the Vose residence was Orson Pratt. So detailed was Brigham's recollection of this meeting that years later he remembered Pratt was seated to his left and that they were both leaning back in their chairs. Suddenly Brigham leaned forward and placed his hand on Pratt's knee and confided to him the insight he had just received—Brigham told Pratt that he knew for certain that the keys to the kingdom were right there with the church.

The six gathered Apostles were galvanized by Brigham's words. Brigham urged that they must return immediately to Nauvoo and assume leadership of the church. The Apostles travelled first by train to Albany on the new railroad link and then headed west by stage and steamboat via Buffalo, Chicago, and Galena. And on August 6 they arrived in Nauvoo to find a scene of doubt, confusion, and disarray.

Most of the Saints were overcome with grief at the loss of Smith, and the church was rudderless. On Brigham's recent campaign swing back through the East, he had made it a point to stop at Kirtland. There he had been dismayed to find coldness and indifference to Smith. Following the dissension in Kirtland back in the late 1830s, a new religion had splintered from the main body of the Church of Jesus Christ of Latter-day Saints. Similar to but independent of Smith's church, this new Kirtland religious sect had taken over the temple there and renounced Smith as a divinely inspired prophet. The splintered sect called itself the Old Standard Church of Christ. The chief dissidents in Kirtland had formed it: Luke and Lyman Johnson, John F. Boynton, and Roger Orton, all excommunicated former elders.

The very same pattern now asserted itself in Nauvoo, under dissidents William Law, Robert D. Foster, and other disaffected and excommunicated elders. When they had attacked the doctrine of polygamy and published the *Nauvoo Expositor* denouncing Smith and his leadership, Law and

Foster had formed their own sect. But that sect, like its predecessor in Kirtland, did not attract large numbers of Saints to defect to it, nor did it ever become a major religion. Brigham and his five fellow Apostles encountered a much bigger problem when they arrived in Nauvoo in early August—the bid for power made by Smith's former chief ministerial counselor, Sidney Rigdon.

An ambitious man who had once been Smith's chief adjutant and leading orator, Rigdon had decamped to Pittsburgh a few years earlier and taken over a branch of the church there. Disaffected with the doctrine of polygamy, just like William Law and his fellow dissenters in Nauvoo, and thus at odds with Smith for the past few years, Rigdon now sought to take over leadership of the church, claiming that the Saints needed to choose a new "guardian" for their church—and that he was just the man for this new role. Nauvoo High Council president William Marks backed Rigdon's bid for power.

As is usual when a leader dies, creating a power vacuum, there were many contenders who wanted to take up Smith's mantle. But Rigdon moved quickly and initially seemed poised to grab control. Marks had scheduled a conference for August 8 to settle this leadership question. Rigdon had pushed hard for this conference to convene before Brigham and the other Apostles could arrive in Nauvoo, but his plan collapsed when they arrived on August 6. The following day they sat down with Marks and Rigdon, and all agreed that the important general conference the next day would decide the issue of church leadership.

The following morning at the general conference Rigdon spoke for two hours straight. As a long-time Saint, a convert from the early days, he had a sure grasp of *The Book of Mormon* and of the history of Mormon suffering and oppression in New York, in Ohio, in Missouri, and now in Illinois. Based on his years as Smith's key advisor and confidant, he made a strong case for his appointment to head up the church, based on his managerial experience and sure grasp of church history. Rigdon did not base his claim to church leadership on Mormon doctrine and theology, but instead put himself forward as the new "guide" the young religion needed and a man worthy to be Smith's "spokesman." But having broken with Smith on recent doctrine, and especially on the controversial practice of polygamy, Rigdon advocated a return to the doctrine practiced in the early years in New York and in Ohio, before any dissension set in.

That afternoon Brigham took to the podium and made one of the most famous speeches in Mormon history, emphasizing Smith's recent appointment of the Quorum of Twelve to the pinnacle of church leadership. Brigham pointed out that as the senior Apostle he held a special place within that leadership. Giving free rein to his caustic tendencies, he mocked Rigdon's speech, asking the congregation whether they desired an organized church or one led by a "Spokesman, Cook, and Bottle Washer."

Brigham then cited the theological authority and eminence Smith had vested in the Twelve Apostles and his grant to them of "the keys to the Kingdom." Brigham mentioned that only the Apostles had received the "Second Endowment" and of late only they had been gathered into Smith's inner circle. In thunderous tones, Brigham assured the congregation that only the Apostles could ensure the congregation's passage into heaven as kings and queens, in keeping with the promise underlying the Mormon endowment ceremony established by Smith years earlier. Saying that the Apostles would oversee the completion of the Nauvoo Temple and of Nauvoo House, Brigham promised the congregation that if Nauvoo proved untenable for the Saints, he would lead them to their proper endowment in the wilderness.

After Brigham spoke, the overwhelming majority of the congregation voted in favor of the Apostles' leading the church. In doing so, the gathered Saints were putting their seal of approval on the primacy of

the priesthood, the sacredness of the temple, the promise of the endowment, and the supreme authority of the Apostles. With near unanimity,
the Saints dismissed Rigdon's claim to leadership. Disappointed, Rigdon
would return to Pittsburgh, where his splinter church eventually dis-
solved from lack of members.

Ironically, though Ridgon had announced his wish to fill the role as
Smith's new "spokesman," many in the congregation later claimed that
Brigham was the one who spoke that day in the voice and intonation
of Joseph Smith. Others went so far as to claim that Brigham appeared
to morph into the person of Smith. Smith was far slighter in build and
quite a bit shorter than Brigham. What people no doubt saw was
Brigham's transformation into a powerful orator and charismatic leader
as he stepped into the shoes of the original Mormon prophet.

It was vintage Brigham that he proceeded cautiously but ruled firmly
in his new role. He did not cast himself in Smith's image as a divine
prophet who had communicated directly with God and conveyed God's
revelations. Though later he would show imperious tendencies, Brigham
was not given to self-aggrandizement in the early days of his ascent to
leadership of the church. In his all-important inaugural speech, Brigham
underscored that the source of his power as leader derived from his
senior position among the Apostles. He asserted that the continued
guidance from God that the church required would come collectively
through the heaven-sent authority vested in the Apostles, based on their
deep knowledge of church doctrine and theology. Thus Brigham solid-
ified his preeminent leadership position without undermining what
harmony remained within the church.

Brigham had to handle relations with the Smith family diplomatically. Joseph Smith's widow Emma had resented Brigham ever since
Brigham backed her husband's announcement of the doctrine of plural
marriage. An even greater challenge was Brigham's relationship with
Smith's only surviving brother, William.

Although William was an original Apostle, he had refused the first major assignment given the Apostles by his brother Joseph when he adamantly disdained to go to England, preach church doctrine, and gather converts. Now, soon after his brother's death, William started to hint that he, as a Smith, should lead the church, adding that his nephew Joseph III, at the time eleven years old, was the prophet's natural successor. Presumably William should lead the church until Joseph was old enough to take charge. William clashed with Brigham and the Apostles on the question of church leadership and eventually left Nauvoo, alleging that Brigham had threatened his life.

Another threat to Brigham's leadership arose from a young lawyer named James Strang, a recent convert. He produced a letter he claimed Smith had given him nine days before his assassination, appointing Strang the new leader of the church and instructing him to "gather" the church to southwestern Wisconsin. But the Apostles examined the letter and promptly excommunicated Strang. In their considered collective judgment, the letter was completely bogus. After establishing his own splinter church, Strang managed to convert some of the Smith family to his cause and gained other adherents by opposing polygamy, a doctrine many Mormons still found difficult.

Eventually Strang did establish a community in Voree, Wisconsin, but then shortly thereafter he moved it to Beaver Island, Michigan, the largest island in Lake Michigan. There Strang set himself up as the leader of what he called the Reorganized Church of Jesus Christ of Latter-day Saints. In time, his church had five hundred followers, but Strang alienated a good many of them when he had himself crowned king and, reversing his previous stance, embraced polygamy. After claiming that he was the heir to Smith's divine inspiration and prophetic and visionary powers, Strang as king issued a dress code for women. When two women refused to follow this code, Strang had their husbands flogged. In retaliation, the two husbands, after briefly biding their time, shot

Strang in the back in 1856. So he, like Smith, was murdered, partly because of his own provocation.

Other assorted challenges to Brigham's authority developed, but he managed to cope with all of them. Lyman Wight, an early convert to the church who had ordained Sidney Rigdon to the priesthood years ago, and who himself had been ordained an Apostle in 1841 while Brigham was away in England, refused to accept Brigham's elevation to overall leadership of the church. Like Rigdon, Wight broke with the church. Wight led a community of followers to Texas, but like Ridgon's new religion in Pittsburgh, Wight's church in Texas would dwindle in membership and finally dissolve.

In contrast—to the dismay of many enemies of Mormonism working to obstruct the Mormon church and force the Latter-day Saints out of Illinois, the Saints in Nauvoo found continuity and strength in the stable leadership provided by Brigham at the head of the Quorum of Twelve Apostles. His light-touch-but-firm-hand method of leadership in the early years (which would give way to despotism only as he aged) provided exactly the leadership the church needed to flourish. Still, the Saints in Illinois continued to meet with hostility and aggression from outsiders—often provoked by the Mormons' insistence on polygamy and sometimes exacerbated by their persistence in political lobbying and deal-making. This state of affairs would test Brigham very early on in his leadership of the church.

CHAPTER 15

HISTORY

REPEATS ITSELF

Brigham showed his extraordinary ability as a leader right from the start. The wisest move he made was his refusal to seek vengeance upon the killers of Joseph and Hyrum Smith. Brigham counseled acceptance of fate rather than revenge. The enemies of the Mormons had always objected to the political power that Mormons wielded as a unified voting bloc and to any hint of Mormon aggression. As far back as the formation of the Danites in Missouri and also in Nauvoo, where the Nauvoo Legion was the city militia under Mormon control, Brigham had never advocated retaliatory aggression from the Saints. Regrettably, in his later years in the Utah Territory, Brigham would arrogantly and foolishly abandon his non-aggression policy and precipitate trouble for Mormons in general and for himself in particular—culminating in his removal from political office.

Back in Missouri in 1838, when circumstances were deteriorating for the Mormons, Rigdon had given a fiery Independence Day speech advocating Mormon retaliation. At the time Joseph Smith had agreed with Rigdon, but later he came to look upon retaliation with a wary eye, believing it would lead to Mormon extinction at the hands of the vast majority arrayed against them. Brigham followed Smith's later, wiser policy of non-aggression—until his meltdown in the later years out West.

The aggression against the Mormons back in the late 1830s in Missouri had escalated to massacres, including several perpetrated by the official state militia following Governor Lilburn W. Boggs's extermination order. In his initial wisdom, Brigham Young, much like later leaders of persecuted minorities Mahatma Gandhi and Martin Luther King Jr., recognized the futility of fighting violence with violence when outnumbered. His later abandonment of this policy in Utah had disastrous effects, as will be seen.

For now, Brigham was wise. Instead of launching any attempts to seek vengeance on the renegade militiamen who had murdered Joseph and Hyrum Smith, instead of organizing any forceful Mormon militia designed to fight for the Mormon cause, Brigham counseled his people in Nauvoo to complete the Nauvoo Temple and Nauvoo House, Joseph Smith's two favorite projects. Brigham wanted the Saints to set an example of quiet and peaceful determination. He urged the Saints to take their spiritual and religious duties with the highest degree of seriousness, and to spruce up their homes and gardens. This would show hostile outsiders in Illinois that Mormons were a peaceful, self-sufficient, and industrious people seeking only to live according to the principles set forth by Jesus Christ.

In addition, Brigham and the other Apostles made clear that the mission of the church was not changed. Going forward, it would espouse the same beliefs and practice the same virtues that it had championed while Smith was alive. The assignment for all Mormons was to carry on as before, placing their trust in God and performing their expected duties. The stability that resulted from Brigham's wise, calm approach to leadership saved the church Joseph Smith had founded. Just as Brigham had handled the various aspirants to church leadership with restrained equanimity, thereby preserving institutional harmony and stability, so, too, did he implement a measured and temperate response to continued non-Mormon aggression from without. The enemies of Mormonism had misjudged the new religion as a passing cult dependent upon the presence of Joseph Smith as leader. With Brigham in charge, these detractors and enemies came to realize that the Mormons were substantial and were here to stay. This realization prompted many non-Mormons in Illinois to resume their efforts to expel the Mormons from the state.

But Brigham was wise and rational. In the face of resumed and ever-escalating hostility, he neither panicked nor advocated that the Mormons pull up stakes and leave the state with their tail between their legs. On the contrary, he advanced a shrewd two-pronged program. First, the Mormons would continue to build in Nauvoo as they sought to achieve guarantees of sanctuary from government officials all the way up to the state governor and the state legislators. Second, at the same time, they would discreetly explore the option of undertaking a mass exodus to a better and safer—because far more isolated—location in the virgin territories to the west, possibly in California or in the Oregon Territory.

Both of these locations were then undergoing settlement by early pioneers, but because of the dangers of the trip west across the plains, the Rockies, and the deserts, the pioneers were so far comparatively few in number. The western territories were mainly isolated, remote, sparsely populated, and lightly governed. Brigham considered such conditions ideal for settlement by the Saints, as had Smith years earlier when the trouble in Illinois originally arose and the Saints first contemplated relocation to the west. Now Brigham set about considering these western territories more seriously, even as he continued to build a lasting Mormon legacy in Nauvoo.

In executing this two-pronged policy, Brigham would rely on shrewd diplomacy rather than stark confrontation—which could lead to violence. Not long after the assassination of the Smith brothers, in the summer of 1845, Warsaw, the neighboring town to Nauvoo and an old source of anti-Mormon sentiment, passed a town council resolution calling for the expulsion of all Mormons from Illinois. When the resolution proved ineffective, the town organized an unsanctioned anti-Mormon militia under the leadership of Colonel Levi Williams. The goal of this rogue militia was to force the Mormons out of the state or else to slaughter them and raze their communities. But before this inhumane and reckless project could gain momentum, Governor Thomas Ford stepped in, dispatching General John J. Hardin and an official state militia to counter the vigilantes and disband them. As a result, the threat to the Mormons passed and peace prevailed—for the time being.

But only a few months later, around the beginning of autumn 1845, trouble flared up again. Anti-Mormon agitators torched twenty-nine Mormon homes in the town of Morley, burning them to the ground. A few weeks later an anti-Mormon rally in Quincy threatened more violence, stirring up mobs to expel the Saints from Illinois. Then, in October, representatives from nine counties near Hancock County convened a meeting that concluded by issuing a statement declaring it was too late to negotiate a living arrangement with the Mormons in Hancock County and therefore no other option existed but removal of all Mormons from the state.

In response, Brigham directed the Saints to complete the main task he had laid out: to finish building the Nauvoo Temple. This would not only honor the memory of Joseph Smith but would show that the Mormons did not leave any desolation in their wake. Work on the temple progressed at a rapid pace. With equal rapidity, Brigham and the Apostles—taking a realistic view of Mormon prospects in Illinois—stepped up planning for an exodus from the state.

Just as Brigham had perceived sooner than others that life in Missouri would be impossible for the Saints, here again in Illinois he had taken the first tentative steps toward an exodus early on, in anticipation of the worst possible scenario. Back in April, Brigham had written to President James K. Polk requesting help in relocating the Saints to the far western territories, a long distance from the states. Leaving no stone unturned, at the same time Brigham had also written to the governors of each state in the country—except for Missouri and Illinois—asking if the Saints might find sanctuary there. Stephen A. Douglas, a congressman from Illinois, urged Brigham to take the Saints to Vancouver Island in the Pacific Northwest. Illinois Governor Ford urged Brigham to move out to California instead, to a vacant area where the Mormons could settle and set up an independent government of their own. Both Douglas and Ford had helped the Saints in the past, but now, because of continued violence against the Mormons, both high-ranking state officials wanted the Mormon problem to go away, and so they urged a mass exodus.

By this time, Brigham and the Apostles had pretty much made up their minds to migrate west. They focused on what was called "the Great Salt Lake Valley." Brigham had gathered all the intelligence then available about this region. He and the Apostles had studied maps of it and all nearby territories. They had obtained what reports there were from trappers, military personnel, and explorers. Here, another of the three great founders of the American West mentioned earlier, John C. Frémont, proved extremely helpful to the Mormons through the accounts and maps he had left behind of the territories he had explored, including the Great Salt Lake Valley. So serious were Mormon plans to migrate there that Brigham and the Apostles decided to send an exploratory company of fifteen hundred men to prepare the region for the great migration to follow. This exploratory expedition never took place, for unfortunate reasons.

In December of 1845, anti-Mormon activity escalated to such an extent that Governor Ford ordered the official state militia under General John J. Hardin to take control of Nauvoo and impose what amounted to martial law. Such oppression was unacceptable to Brigham and the Apostles. And there was also a threat that Brigham might be arrested on a charge that the Saints were harboring a counterfeiting operation run by a gang of river traffickers hiding out in Nauvoo. To top even this threat, Governor Ford informed Brigham and the Apostles of a rumor that federal troops in St. Louis were preparing to intercept the Mormons and wipe them out. This rumor appears to have been more ruse than fact. But it had the desired effect. Feeling even more imperiled, the Saints made hasty plans to move out of Nauvoo earlier than their original projected departure date of spring 1846.

Brigham and the Apostles continued to implement their two-pronged agenda. In the midst of the crisis, the upper rooms of the Nauvoo Temple were finished, and Brigham immediately instituted services there and began to grant the endowments and celestial marital sealings so long awaited by the faithful. "Celestial sealing" was a Mormon ceremony that "sealed" a bride permanently to her husband, even unto eternity, even when the marriage was polygamous. Such celestially sealed married couples could expect, as part of their endowment, to spend eternity as a king and queen in the bridegroom's "celestial family." By instituting Temple rituals, Brigham showed the Saints that nothing could come before their religion or sidetrack the theological mission of their church. Brigham conducted most of these religious services at night. During the day he worked in the Temple, administering church business and supervising the final stages of construction. He stayed at the Temple around the clock, sleeping in a small room prepared for him on the upper floors.

By day he mainly directed a massive effort by the Saints to prepare for an exodus from Nauvoo that winter, even though winter travel would make the journey harder and more dangerous. Instead of awaiting the spring thaw, the Saints were determined to vacate Illinois as soon as possible. The reason was simple: the violence against them continued to escalate and the jurisdiction of the militia over them—martial law, in effect—was too heavy a weight for the community of Saints to bear. In early winter, Brigham, the Apostles, and other church elders met with a contingent of Illinois state officials, including Governor Ford and Congressman Douglas, and worked out a formal signed agreement for the Saints to depart.

The Saints immediately began to make open arrangements to leave. The haste of the evacuation visited unwanted hardships on them. Brigham had the *Nauvoo Neighbor* run articles directing the faithful on how to pack for the exodus and what they would need by way of tools and provisions to make the daunting journey. But these articles triggered unethical traders and real estate speculators to commence buying Mormon homes, properties, and other valuables at distressed prices, knowing the Saints had neither time nor inclination to enter lengthy negotiations.

Quickly realizing what was going on, Brigham told his followers not to fret about financial loss but to carry out the necessary arrangements to make the exodus possible. The Saints ended up selling many possessions far below market value in order to secure what they most needed to make their historic trek to the west. In exchange for their possessions, the Saints took in money, oxen, horses, cattle, tools, wagons, fish hooks and nets, hunting rifles, and nonperishable food stuffs that would be needed both in transit and when they reached the Great Salt Lake Valley.

Because his confidence was so deep, based as it was on faith, Brigham decided to leave at the worst time, in deepest winter. The growing unrest, turmoil, and chaos in Nauvoo had become unbearable. Increased violence, arson, and other forms of hostile attacks on the Mormons had become insufferable, as had chafing under the harsh and often arbitrary martial law imposed by the Illinois state militia under General Hardin.

On Groundhog Day, February 2, 1846, Brigham directed the Saints to procure boats and hold them in readiness to transport the wagons and teams across the wide Mississippi. Two days later, he was loading his own family's wagon in preparation for the departure. Brigham knew that the plains would be frigid, the rivers and creeks frozen, and the mountains possibly impassable with snow. Still he directed that all be made ready for the exodus. On February 9, a fire broke out on the roof of the newly finished Nauvoo Temple. Acting quickly to organize a bucket brigade, Brigham's cousin Willard Richards managed to douse the fire before it could spread widely.

Six days later, the Nauvoo police force, a Mormon institution under the direction of Hosea Stout, had assembled a serendipitous collection of flatboats and other light vessels on the Nauvoo flats. The Mississippi had not yet iced over, as it would weeks later to such a degree that Mormon wagons making the journey later rolled across the thick ice and into Iowa. But by the time the river iced over, Brigham had gone.

Utilizing the small haphazard flotilla the Nauvoo police had assembled, Brigham and his family crossed the river on Sunday, February 15, 1846, in the vanguard of the great Mormon exodus to the western wilderness. The Youngs were accompanied by their cousin Willard Richards and his family and by their faithful old friend George A. Smith. Leading this vast migration would be Brigham Young's signature achievement.

CHAPTER 16

THE GREAT

· • ·

EXODUS

Brigham planned the exodus brilliantly. Knowing what he did about the terrain ahead, he broke the journey into manageable segments. And drawing upon the experience of the arduous trek of over a thousand miles to Missouri with Zion's Camp in 1834, Brigham heeded the lessons he had learned on that journey under Joseph Smith. (Brigham drew a parallel between the two great treks by referring to the western exodus of the 1840s by the title of Israel's Camp.) Brigham convinced the Apostles and elders that the journey to the far West would only be successful if it were undertaken in what amounted to a relay over the course of two arduous years. Taking a page from Joseph Smith's direction of Zion's camp, Brigham first organized his wagon trains into units based on a military-style chain of command. His next priority was to set up a string of camps across the state of Iowa. These camps would serve as way stations to bring his people to the banks of the Missouri River, where it marks the boundary between Iowa and Nebraska.

The first order of business was to establish a base camp, as mountain climbers do today. Brigham established the Saints' base camp miles into Iowa at a place called Sugar Creek. Sugar Creek was only a short distance from Nauvoo, but Brigham wanted to go ahead and acclimate his people quickly to the hardships of camp life, and he wanted the base camp to be close enough to Nauvoo that he could communicate with his brother Joseph during his stay there. Also, he wanted to establish from the beginning the leapfrogging pattern that the Mormons would use for the rest of their journey west, going from one camp to the next, then to the next, breaking the long trek into manageable segments. Before Brigham crossed the Mississippi, he placed Joseph at the head of a committee of five men in charge of overseeing the sale of Mormon properties in Nauvoo, including the Nauvoo Temple and Nauvoo House hotel. Joseph Young was also to help later pioneers prepare their provisions and wagons for the journey west.

Mormon records indicate that nine babies were born the first night of the encampment at Sugar Creek. There were also howling prairie winds and bitter coldness to contend with. That winter of 1846 turned severe, and the Saints soon had to cope with temperatures that plummeted as low as twenty degrees below zero. The one blessing from this was that the Mississippi froze over and later wagons leaving Nauvoo could cross the river on the thick ice. No more flatboats or ferries were needed, so passage across the river was easier and faster.

Problems that would confront Brigham throughout this massive move west cropped up immediately. Right from the start, life in encampments proved too hard for some of his followers. Recognizing the potential of such disaffected people to hinder the entire operation, and realizing that some were simply not cut out for pioneering life, Brigham let them go. Many turned their wagons around and headed back to

Nauvoo and from there to settlements in established church branches in the East and the Midwest. As Brigham saw quickly, circumstances in Iowa that winter were simply too difficult and stressful for many people. Disaffection would increase as the challenges continued to mount throughout the push westward. Yet Brigham managed, despite his frustration, to handle the discouraged pioneers and their problems.

One key to the ultimate success of the exodus was the military-style system Brigham imposed on the wagon trains. Joseph Smith had instituted similar measures when Brigham was one of his chief aides on Zion's Camp, but on a much smaller scale. Now Brigham organized his people into units consisting of fifty families, which he then broke into smaller units of ten families each. Every ten-family unit had a captain at its head to supervise, maintain order and discipline, and pass out assignments such as standing guard or herding the livestock or kitchen duty or procuring food by hunting or foraging. There was also much livestock to be cared for and guarded.

Because of the history of violence against the Mormons, Brigham posted armed guards to patrol the outskirts of the wagon trains and to guard the permanent encampments and also the makeshift camps that were pitched every night in transit. The details of how Brigham would lead the exodus west leaked out, and the press made them known far and wide, increasing the risk of attack by anti-Mormon mobs and mounted vigilantes. Brigham had learned from the mob attacks against Zion's Camp in Missouri, and on this great western exodus he was determined to ensure his people's safety, by any means he could muster, while they were in transit and highly vulnerable.

The plans Brigham had made in advance worked well as the Latter-day Saints moved across Iowa, despite the defections from some of his discouraged followers. As the exodus moved west, Brigham would first set up a permanent encampment, a way station like the one at Sugar Creek. Then he would send out a pioneer corps a good distance ahead, usually about a hundred miles or so. This advance unit consisted of able-bodied men whose task it was to pick the next site for a way station and construct a kind of primitive village there for continued use by the wagon trains of pioneers passing through later.

When these villages were completed, the advance party would plant crops. That way, food would be available to those following later. This process explains how the Saints established the temporary communities of Garden Grove and Mount Pisgah deeper into Iowa to serve as way stations as the trail took shape that would lead to the banks of the Missouri River and, across it, to the plains of Nebraska. These temporary communities were resting places where the pioneers could recoup their strength and repair their resolve, and also laboratories where, in the building of these small villages, the pioneers sharpened their colonizing skills for the larger job of building a permanent settlement in the Great Salt Lake Valley.

Two weeks after Brigham crossed the Mississippi with his family, everything was ready for the first push west from Sugar Creek in early March. The day before the planned departure Brigham endured a painful attack of rheumatism. He had to remain behind temporarily and rest. So, in his stead, he appointed Heber Chase Kimball to explain to the Saints gathered for Sunday morning services the importance of moving on. It was imperative to push forward to the next big encampment at Garden Grove, 150 miles west of Nauvoo. Kimball carefully laid out the instructions for the pioneers to follow.

At noon the wagons started to move out, with Kimball's wagon in the lead. The wagons lined up in a row along a road chosen and prepared nearly a week earlier by an advance caravan of sixteen wagons under the direction of Bishop George Miller. Four days behind Miller came a crew of one hundred men, roughly the equivalent of the Army Corps of Engineers or navy Seabees, under the command of Colonel Stephen Markham of the Nauvoo Legion. Their job was to clear the road and make it more easily passable for the main wagon train under Heber Kimball to follow. This advance crew of workmen even built small primitive bridges across creeks and streams. Behind them, a unit of one hundred riflemen on horseback patrolled on each side of the road. The riflemen worked in shifts under the leadership of Hosea Stout, who had headed up the Nauvoo police force. For added safety and protection, there was an artillery force of another one hundred men under Colonel John Scott backing up the armed outriders.

Brigham never hesitated to compare this exodus to the one in the Bible, often referring to the Mormon march to the West as Israel's Camp. Contemporary observers made the same comparison; written accounts testify that anyone observing two or three thousand men, women, and children trekking across the plains, along with hundreds of animals tethered to the tailgates of their wagons, would think immediately of the Israelites. These were the animals for which the departing pioneers had undersold their household goods and even, in many cases, their Nauvoo houses. In preparing for this long journey, Brigham, mindful of morale, had included a brass band that not only roused the sleeping encampment every morning but also played music every night for entertainments, including dances. The dances provided an outlet for tension, and quite frequently the pioneers would break into songfests. These things boosted the Saints' spirits.

The passage across Iowa took three and a half months. Brigham and the wagon train arrived in what is today Council Bluffs at the western extreme of Iowa on June 14. There they stopped on the eastern banks of the Missouri River. Along the way, besides stopping at the big way station at Garden Grove, where they arrived on April 25, and at Mount Pisgah, where they arrived on May 25, the wagon train had stopped earlier at Richardson Point, fifty-five miles from Nauvoo, on March 7; at the Chariton River, where they arrived on March 22; and at Locust River, reached on April 6.

All had gone smoothly; the journey had been well-organized and well-planned. Along the way, Brigham had directed the Saints to take temporary work where they could find it. So the pioneering Saints had helped settlers with their carpentry, wood chopping, clearing, and other farming chores, hiring themselves out for cash or more commonly for barter of provisions and supplies to ease their harsh transit across the plains.

Brigham laid down the law to those men who shirked duty or complained too much. Only a few days west of Sugar Creek, he told shirkers who didn't want to contribute their all to the common good and to the success of the mission to turn back. He knew the journey would become progressively harder, both in terms of the terrain to be crossed and the psychological and physical deprivation to be endured. Because Brigham brooked no malingering and tolerated no deadbeats, nearly every day wagons peeled off and turned back. But the main body of the wagon train went on.

It is not hard to understand why some people abandoned the trek and turned back. Death was a constant companion along the trail. Some pioneers died from fatigue, others from fevers, pneumonia, dysentery, whooping cough, measles, and other forms of disease, and still others perished from simply not having enough to eat. Malnutrition was a serious problem. Food and game were hard to come by in the middle of nowhere in the depths of a harsh winter. So many Saints died along the trail that funeral rites were conducted and burials carried out every week.

Brigham decided to set up a large encampment in Florence, Nebraska, just across the Missouri river from Council Bluffs, Iowa. Today, Florence has been incorporated into Omaha, Nebraska, but back then it actually preceded Omaha into existence as a frontier settlement thanks to the Mormons, whose advance scouting party arrived there as early as January of 1846, a month or so before Brigham left Nauvoo in the middle of February.

The original plan devised by Brigham and the Apostles had called for the Saints to press on across Nebraska, not to dig in anywhere along the trail but to keep leapfrogging forward. Yet when Brigham's wagon train reached Council Bluffs, Iowa, on June 14, he altered his plans. There would be no temporary village set up by an advance pioneer corps fifty or a hundred miles farther west into Nebraska to which Brigham's lead wagon train would advance within days.

Instead, following Brigham's orders, the Mormons expanded the Florence settlement all during the summer and fall of 1846 in order to dig in for a winter stay. They even built the famous Florence Mill, among the earliest mills in Nebraska and destined to become part of Mormon lore. Powered by water, the mill provided both flour and lumber in what became known as Winter Quarters. The mill enabled the Mormons to cope better with the adverse winter conditions during their prolonged stay in Florence that first winter of 1846–1847. And it would serve the same function for future wagon trains of Mormon pioneers wintering at Florence for several years to come.

Brigham had altered the original plan and elected to build the substantial settlement at Florence—a functioning town, really—because of what he had learned on the arduous crossing of Iowa over the course of three and a half harrowing winter months, and also because a political situation arose that he thought could benefit his church. He and the Saints would bide their time in Florence while better preparations were made for the even more challenging journey ahead. First would come the challenge of crossing the sparse plains and badlands of Nebraska. Then would follow the daunting climb into the Rockies to traverse the mountain passes leading down to the Great Salt Lake Valley. But first Brigham intended to capitalize on the political opportunity suddenly presented to him.

CHAPTER 17

WINTER
• • •
QUARTERS

Besides Brigham's correct intuition that additional planning and preparation had to be made in order to successfully complete the trek to the Far West, another development provided him with the opportunity to place his people in a shrewd position vis à vis the political dangers they had endured so far in their history. This development was the outbreak of the Mexican-American War, and the strategy Brigham used to seize that opportunity was the formation of what became known as the Mormon Battalion.

A month before Brigham left Nauvoo, he had instructed his nephew, Jesse C. Little, a merchant based in the East and in charge of the church branches there, to take every advantage possible to gain government assistance for the migration west. In Philadelphia, Little met an idealistic and humanitarian young Irishman named Thomas L. Kane. Kane saw the Mormons as an admirable people unfairly oppressed. He resolved to help them and accompanied Little to Washington, D.C., to lobby the president on their behalf. That Kane's father had close political connections to President James K. Polk wouldn't hurt the Mormon cause.

At first the Mormon aspiration was to have Little secure a government contract for them to build a chain of forts for the federal government along the route known as the Oregon Trail. This trail stretched from parts of what is now Kansas all the way to present-day Oregon. It connected the banks of the Missouri River to the shores of the Pacific Ocean. Originally a narrow path for foot and hoof, the Oregon Trail eventually expanded to accommodate large-wheel wagons and, before the intercontinental expansion of the railroad, provided the route for four hundred thousand pioneers to reach and settle the Far West. But before Little could secure a contract for the Mormons to build forts along the Oregon Trail, war broke out in May of 1846 between the United States and Mexico for control of Texas and California.

This presented a more immediate opportunity for the Saints to prove their loyalty and usefulness to the nation. President James K. Polk sought to ensure America's transcontinental expansion, and he knew that foreign powers, especially the British, had designs on northern California and the Pacific Northwest. He also sought to ensure the independence of Texas from Mexico. The president harbored the fear that the Mormons were so thoroughly disaffected with the United States federal government because of its failure to protect them from the violence in Missouri and in Illinois that they would align themselves with the British or with another European power, or even with the Mexicans against the interests of the Texans. This state of affairs provided the Mormons with leverage that amounted to a powerful negotiating tool.

The upshot was the formation of the now famous Mormon Battalion. Polk, who wanted to be sure that the Mormons fought on the U.S. side of the war, asked Brigham to raise five hundred recruits to help the United States Army prevail in Texas and most especially in California. This request pleased Brigham for two reasons. It guaranteed much-needed cash to the Saints from the army payroll of the Mormon Battalion, and it assured the Saints of safe passage to their sanctuary in the desert.

Brigham was killing two birds with one stone—raising funds to support the exodus and cementing a friendly relationship with the federal government. But of course there were also drawbacks, large and small. The big disadvantage was that five hundred young, skilled, and able Mormon men needed by Brigham to forge the way to the Great Salt Lake Valley as an advance pioneer corps would instead be in the employ of the United States Army fighting for control of California and Texas. A smaller problem was that grumblings arose because Brigham, as head of the church, commandeered the federal pay of the Mormon soldiers and used it to build up Winter Quarters. Some soldiers and their wives and families particularly resented the reports that Brigham used their pay to reimburse himself as contractor on the construction of the Florence Mill. This lining his own pockets at the expense of the Mormon Battalion soldiers set a precedent; in later years, Brigham would be accused of indulging in assorted sharp practices for his own gain, often involving the appropriation and disposal of church resources and funds.

The significant historical fact is that the five hundred members of the Mormon Battalion would be transported to California as soldiers at government expense, that the U.S. government, in return, would officially sanction Mormon camps on Indian land in Nebraska, that the government would permit Mormon use of grassland for grazing and of timber for building, and, lastly, that the federal government would not impede Mormon plans to settle outside federal jurisdiction in the Great Salt Lake Valley when the wagon trains resumed their trek in the spring of 1847, a year later. The agreement with the federal government showed Brigham at his managerial and diplomatic best; he had demonstrated adeptness at political maneuvering in the interests of his church and his people.

Brigham went from camp to camp recruiting his young male followers to join the army. Mounting wagons or standing on high ground, he spoke eloquently to hastily gathered crowds about how vital to the interests of the church Mormon service in the army of their country would be, and how it would reap enormous benefits for all the Saints in their westward quest for political and religious asylum. Brigham spoke right alongside the official recruiter for the U.S. Army, Captain James Allen. Allen was there to recruit the five hundred Mormon volunteers on behalf of General Stephen F. Kearney, the commander of the Army of the West, headquartered at Fort Leavenworth.

Brigham's efforts yielded rapid results. Accompanied by Captain Allen, he traveled across the breadth of the Iowa plains to all the Mormon camps strung out between the Mississippi and the Missouri Rivers and delivered the message about recruitment. It is a testament to Brigham's persuasive oratory and leadership skills that within weeks the five hundred young Mormon recruits were in hand. Having put their personal affairs in order and bid farewell to family and friends, all five hundred met at the Council Bluffs encampment and left on July 20 for Fort Leavenworth, where they arrived on August 30.

There they were sworn into the army, equipped, quickly trained, and dispatched to San Diego, California. Their march along the Santa Fe Trail was quite grueling and possibly the longest in the history of the U.S. Army up to that time. The Mormon Battalion served with distinction for a year, until July of 1847. Among its other accomplishments, the battalion helped General Kearney thwart John C. Frémont's rogue takeover attempt in California, the one that later cost him his chance at the presidency as the first candidate, ever, of the newly formed Republican Party. The battalion also built historic Fort Moore in what is today downtown Los Angeles. It's worth noting that twenty-two of the Mormon recruits died from disease or other natural causes during their year of service.

While the Mormon Battalion served in the army during the winter of 1846–1847, Brigham accomplished much in Winter Quarters. In addition to building the Florence Mill, he set up an internal mail system all along the line of the Mormon encampments stretching back through Iowa to Nauvoo. He also supervised the organization of a new missionary expedition to England and the overall organization of church efforts there, especially the emigration to America of new converts. Realizing that he now had sixteen thousand Saints spread out over several hundred miles from Nauvoo to Winter Quarters, he took measures to strengthen internal organization, boost morale, and strengthen resolve.

As a preparatory measure for the remainder of the journey, which would be longer and more daunting than the trek across the Iowa prairie, at Winter Quarters Brigham kept interviewing trappers and explorers who had traversed the lands to the west, trying to gain all the knowledge available about the challenges ahead. Brigham and the Apostles as well as other Mormon elders benefited greatly during this winter from a meeting with the famous Jesuit missionary Father Pierre-Jean De Smet. A few years earlier, Father De Smet had made a long and wide-ranging exploration of the Rockies. He had been quite daring in his travels and gave Brigham and his church associates an emphatic endorsement of the Great Salt Lake Valley, which only confirmed the decision Brigham had reached a year earlier to make that area the site of the new Zion.

In retrospect, Brigham's flexibility in delaying the push across Nebraska until the spring of 1847 proved crucial to the success of the whole enterprise. His discretion in taking more time to prepare for the remaining leg of the journey and his shrewdness in capitalizing on the political and financial benefits offered by the creation of the Mormon Battalion did not in any way mitigate Brigham's iron resolve to push on to the Far West.

More eloquent proof of this cannot be found anywhere than in the great quote from Brigham cited by Francis M. Gibbons in his biography titled *Brigham Young: Modern Moses, Prophet of God*. Huddled over his makeshift desk in the primitive and frigid log cabin at Winter Quarters that Brigham temporarily called home, in the middle of a freezing January during that arctic winter of 1847, he wrote a letter to Charles C. Rich, the elder in charge of the encampment back at Mount Pisgah in Iowa. After telling Charles that he intended to send an advance pioneering corps ahead of the wagon trains in early spring, which he wished Charles to join, Brigham rallied his friend for the task that loomed ahead with the following words: "Gird up your loins, put on your armor, cheer up your heart, and being filled with Almighty faith, prepare for the battle as fast as possible. If you are sick, be made well. If you are weak, be made strong. Shake yourself like a mighty man, make the forest to echo the sound of your voice and the prairies move at your presence."

As Brigham wrote these stirring words, he was engaged on a daily basis in administering to the sick and diseased, conducting burial rites for the dead, providing food and other provisions for those encamped with him, communicating with the Apostles abroad on the English mission, supervising emigration of converts to the United States, and working away feverishly on the final logistics of the spring push to the mountains and to the Great Basin and the great inland salt lake within it.

As Brigham informed Charles C. Rich in the letter quoted above, which rests today in the official church archives, he had organized a pioneering corps to blaze the trail to the Great Salt Lake Valley in early spring. The corps consisted of able-bodied men, mostly young, and possessed of every skill required to clear and mark the trail, draw maps, spell out directions, offer traveling advice, and, once arrived in the desert, to sow a summer crop to sustain the pioneers in the wagon trains to follow.

CHAPTER 18

TO THE GREAT
SALT LAKE VALLEY

In the late winter and early spring of 1847, the sounds of saws and hammers rang out everywhere in Winter Quarters. Brigham had ordered everyone to put the finishing touches on wagons and other equipment and to be ready to move out with the first warm breezes of spring. When some members fell behind in outfitting their wagons, gathering their provisions, and procuring their oxen, Brigham came down hard on them in early March and gave them short and hard deadlines that he personally monitored. He was determined that nothing should go wrong from carelessness or shoddy preparation. He knew this upcoming segment of the journey was going to tax nerves, stress stamina, and challenge mental resolve and physical toughness as the trip across Iowa had not, hard as that had been. As a result of Brigham's laying down the law and imposing strict deadlines, seventy wagons were ready to go by early April, completely loaded and provisioned.

In his planning, Brigham had selected a cadre of hearty souls to form the first wagon train to attempt the sweep across the Nebraska plains, the ascent over the Wyoming mountains, and the rollercoaster trek up, through, and down the narrow canyons of the far Rockies that led into the Great Salt Lake Valley. Besides the young and skillful men Brigham and the Apostles had carefully selected, there were a few others in the advance corps. Only three women came along: Clara Decker, Brigham's plural wife; his brother Lorenzo's wife, Harriet Decker; and Heber Chase Kimball's plural wife, Ellen Sanders. In addition, there were two children. Altogether the wagon train had 148 pioneers. This number was relatively small for a pioneering wagon train, especially in comparison to the larger caravans of Saints that would follow over the next several years. But Brigham wanted to blaze the trail with only the most able; he could not afford the deadweight and whiners who had retarded progress at times during the Iowa crossing.

Besides driving seventy wagons, the small band carried a leather boat and a cannon. The livestock they took included ninety-three horses, fifty-two mules, sixty-six oxen, nineteen cows, seventeen dogs, and a few chickens. Heber Kimball started west on April 5 with half a dozen of his wagons. Brigham stayed behind for one day to attend a church council and impart final instructions for the maintenance and security of Winter Quarters. For added security, he wanted it surrounded by a stockade. Then, on April 6, he and the remainder of the vanguard wagon train moved out and rendezvoused with Heber Kimball and his small band a short distance to the west. Brigham had intended to stay with the wagon train and move west, but he changed his plans when word arrived that Parley Pratt had reached Winter Quarters shortly after Brigham departed. Eager to debrief Parley and hear of progress in England, Brigham rode back to Winter Quarters. There he heard good news from Pratt and was greatly pleased that the Saints and converts in England were faring well.

Brigham had no more rejoined the wagon train at the Elkhorn River than word reached him that John Taylor had arrived at Winter Quarters, also back from his mission to England. Brigham again hastened east to see Taylor. Not only did Taylor confirm Pratt's report of good progress in England, he brought back a substantial sum raised for the church in America by the British Saints. Importantly, Taylor also brought back instruments and equipment that Brigham eagerly wanted for the trek west: two sextants, two barometers, two artificial horizons, one circle of reflection, and one telescope. All this badly needed equipment was boxed up again and transported with Brigham back to the Platte River and the waiting camp. Brigham had prearranged with Heber Kimball to hold the camp at the Platte River, forty-seven miles west of Winter Quarters, so that Brigham and a few other elders who had ridden back to see Taylor could rejoin the wagon train for the push west.

Because they were now traveling through country where Native Americans often felt violated and sometimes turned hostile, and also through country where danger from wild animals lurked, Brigham imposed additional rules on the company. He instituted a strict military hierarchy with himself at the top and with a colonel, a first major, and a second major descending in order of authority; they were above the previously mentioned captains of individual companies consisting of ten wagons each. Brigham also issued firm rules about firearms, which had to be kept loaded and instantly handy at all times. No one was to leave the wagons, and the man in charge of each wagon was to walk beside it at all times. Guards would be placed at night and reveille was at five sharp each morning. In the evening, after a brief prayer service, all but the guards would retire at nine. The noon meal would be cooked ahead of time so it could be consumed in transit without losing any time.

Among the other breakthroughs the Saints made on their trek west was the invention of the odometer, originally called a "roadometer." They devised an ingenious method for measuring distance travelled with a set of wooden cogs attached to the hub of a wagon wheel; the tallied revolutions of the individual cogs were calibrated to the revolution of the bigger wheel and through extrapolation the distance traveled by the circumference of the wagon wheel could be calculated. By this means, the pioneers were able to measure the miles traveled with surprising accuracy. And their calibrations proved incredibly helpful to later pioneers. As the camp moved west, they also posted some primitive signs, which were also helpful to those following later.

At the Platte River, Brigham made a shrewd decision. The camp would follow the north bank of the river, not the more heavily used south bank. As much as possible, Brigham wanted to avoid encounters with the wagon trains originating from Missouri. There were Mormon-haters among these groups, and some were even led by men with a vendetta against the Latter-day Saints. Wagon trains could and did vie for the right of way and for the best camping sites, and Brigham did not want to court conflict that could be avoided. His instincts were vindicated later when the camp reached Fort Laramie and learned that a wagon train under the direction of Lilburn W. Boggs had arrived earlier and spread vicious slanders and lies about Mormons. This was the same Lilburn W. Boggs who had, when governor of Missouri in 1838, issued the infamous extermination order against all Mormons.

Brigham also knew that anti-Mormon elements such as Boggs had incited the Native Americans against the Mormons, and he did not want to confront these indigenous people in any way. When the Saints first met the Pawnees weeks later they were instructed by them not to kill their buffalo. And because Brigham had the forethought to take along negotiators who spoke the languages of the Native Americans, and because when they did reach buffalo country, the Mormons exercised discipline and thrift, and never killed more buffalo than they needed to eat and survive, this issue never proved to be a point of contention. In respecting the hunting grounds of the Native Americans, the Mormons were the exception, not the rule. More often than not, the large wagon trains originating in Missouri would rile the Native Americans by slaughtering buffalo herds indiscriminately, leaving dead and uneaten carcasses scattered on the plains to rot.

Despite these potential trouble spots, the Mormon wagon train progressed with no really daunting challenges until it reached the Loup River. The Loup, a tributary of the Platte, is a notoriously difficult river to cross. It is a swiftly moving stream three or four feet deep and about three hundred yards wide over a soft bed almost like quicksand. At first the Saints tried building a raft to cross it, but this proved impracticable. Then, by scouting farther upstream, they found a more favorable area to ford. After much labor, tripling teams, and reducing loads, the Mormon wagons made it across; but this was a tedious, time-consuming, and backbreaking job.

The Nebraska spring weather proved tricky. Icy winds ripped across the Great Plains and the Saints had to unpack their heavy blankets and outerwear and don gloves and heavy fur caps. The winds kicked up gusts of prairie dust that whirled into their eyes. To add to the discomfort, it was hard to start campfires on these treeless plains for lack of firewood. This meant that the nightly campsites lacked any source of warmth. This problem was solved a little farther on, when the camp finally reached buffalo country and discovered that buffalo droppings made excellent campfires, both for cooking and for heat. Some wits among the Saints made earthy jokes comparing these buffalo chips with the manna from heaven sent to the Israelites.

From the first sighting of a small herd of buffalo on May 1 until a week later on May 8, the landscape changed: those on the wagon train who kept journals reported the prairie alive and moving like the sea with the undulations of vast herds of buffalo covering the land on both sides of the Platte, the thundering force of their hooves sometimes shaking the earth like a quake. Even though the abundance of buffalo solved two problems—supplying food for the pioneers and fuel for their fires—it created another. In passing over the prairie, large herds of buffalo grazed voraciously, stripping the land bare and making it difficult for the pioneers to feed their livestock. The hungry herds of buffalo left nothing to eat for the horses, mules, and oxen pulling the wagons.

When the Saints reached the famous Chimney Rock landmark in western Nebraska, Brigham voiced his displeasure with their conduct along the trail. He mounted a makeshift platform and told the group there was too much complaining and too little seriousness. He decried the arguments he had heard over duties performed or not performed and urged the Saints to pray more and concentrate more on the task at hand. They were now roughly at the halfway point of their journey, and the really difficult part still lay ahead. Brigham wanted more emphasis placed on prayer and on spirituality and less on petty contention. He specifically forbade the playing of checkers, dominoes, and other forms of gambling that he knew were going on in the camp. This was in keeping with Brigham's general policy of religious observance even on the trail, despite its primitive conditions. Generally he did not order travel on Sundays and instead conducted religious services at intervals during the day. On weekdays he ordered prayer sessions either for the whole group together or in the units of fifty or ten. Brigham's tongue-lashing had its proper effect, and seriousness and dedication prevailed.

Once the pioneers arrived across the river from Fort Laramie and all the wagons had been ferried across the river, Brigham ordered the camp to take a respite from travel and regroup. Owned by the American Fur Company, Fort Laramie was a famous old settlement on the Oregon Trail that housed eighteen families and served as a trading post. The manager of the fort was a Frenchman named James Bordeaux with a deep knowledge of the Oregon Trail and of the West in general. Talking to him at length proved helpful to Brigham. Bordeaux spoke highly of the Bear Valley in what is today southern Idaho, and

Brigham filed the information away for possible future expansion of Mormon settlements.

Also at Fort Laramie, a small party of seventeen Mormon pioneers from Alabama and Mississippi, under the leadership of Robert Crow, joined Brigham's wagon train. These Southerners had left their homes in January of 1846, when Brigham first announced that the Saints would forsake Illinois and push westward. They had originally angled their journey for a rendezvous farther west, so when Brigham had delayed the westward movement and stayed in Winter Quarters on the banks of the Missouri, the Southerners had been unable to find the main wagon train. That confusion now remedied, the Crow party joined Brigham's larger group. They brought Brigham news of several members of the Mormon Battalion who had fallen ill and were wintering at Fort Pueblo in what is now Colorado. Concerned for the stricken soldiers, Brigham sent a small party back to Fort Pueblo to assist them when they were well enough to travel, so they, too, could gather in the Great Salt Lake Valley.

The pioneers resumed their journey, following the Oregon Trail. Soon they were in higher altitudes and more challenging terrain. The trail forward was replete with steep climbs and quick descents. As practical and resourceful as ever, Brigham dispatched a small party of men with saws, shovels, pry bars, and rakes to work the trail ahead, smoothing the roadbed and making other improvements. Because some hills were simply too steep for the teams to manage, the wagon train had to add miles to the journey in seeking easier points of transit. The Saints occasionally had to head in the opposite direction from where they wanted to go in order to reach their destination. Yet they pushed onward, grateful that they had brought along heavy clothing to counter the chill mountain air. In addition to the cold in the mountains, sections of southern Wyoming were extremely dusty, with the fields sometimes also infested with crickets so thick on the ground that stepping on them was unavoidable. And the dust infiltrated everything—clothing, blankets, even foodstuffs and cooking utensils.

A few days out from Fort Laramie, the wagon train made its last crossing of the Platte River, near the site of what is today Casper, Wyoming. Here the pioneers planned to use the leather boat they had carted along—to ferry supplies across the river, so that the wagons, lightened of their loads, could float across. Brigham had had the foresight to send a party of men ahead to set up the leather boat. When another wagon train headed for Oregon arrived before Brigham's party, the Mormons enterprisingly offered the boat's services to them, and the future Oregonians accepted. For a fee of $1.50 per load, the Mormons ferried supplies across and earned a total of $34 paid mostly in flour, but some in corn and bacon. When Brigham and the rest of the camp arrived at the river crossing, there was joy as each wagon's meal bag was replenished when the bartered goods were divided fairly among the whole wagon train.

Seeing an opportunity in the heavy pioneer traffic on the Oregon Trail at this difficult juncture, Brigham ordered a large raft to be built. Stripping to the waist, he led a team of men in swiftly constructing a raft sturdy enough to ferry wagons across the river. Brigham, after using the raft to ferry his own wagon train across, ordered a detail of ten men to remain behind at the river and sell rafting services to future wagon trains. In this way, the Mormons operated a profitable ferrying service for several years.

Moving on from this last Platte River crossing, the Saints encountered rough terrain. On June 21, they camped on the banks of the Sweetwater River, opposite the imposing landmark of Independence Rock. This huge granite outcropping is a famous landmark on the Oregon Trail, often described as looking from a distance like a large whale. Longer than six football fields, nearly as wide as three, and forty yards higher than one turned on end, the rock is famous for the number of names carved or painted on it by trappers, travelers, and passing pioneers.

Several of the Mormon pioneers climbed the rock and prayed on its summit, thrilled to see so many names of those who had preceded them.

When the wagon train moved on, Brigham and his followers were delighted to catch their first glimpse of the snow-capped Rockies. Along the trail, Brigham chatted with trappers passing in the opposite direction. As usual, he sought information and advice about the terrain ahead, and he listened carefully to their recommendations of future sites for settlement. Among the legendary mountain men he met were Major Moses Harris and John L. Smith, who kept a well-known trading post on the Bear River near Soda Springs. But the most interesting of these grizzled old mountain men was Jim Bridger. His exploits as a trader, trapper, and trailblazer verged on the fantastic.

Whereas Harris and Smith spoke discouragingly of the Great Salt Lake Valley, citing its lack of timber and its isolation, Bridger spoke of its beauty. Yet he, too, told Brigham that growing grain there would be difficult. He wasn't sure it could be done. Underscoring his skepticism, Bridger offered a thousand dollars for a bushel of corn raised there. Typically optimistic, Brigham told him to wait a while, and he and his followers would show him how to do it. Bridger made a counter-suggestion that Brigham settle in the Cache Valley to the northwest. Brigham listened carefully and noted Bridger's enthusiasm. As it turned out, Bridger's recommendation proved helpful to Brigham in planning a later Mormon settlement. Today Logan is the central city in the Cache Valley and the site of Utah State University. The city's population is heavily Mormon.

Two days after meeting Jim Bridger, on June 30, Brigham connected with Samuel Brannan and two companions who had trekked east to try to convince Brigham to settle in California, as they already had, along with other Mormons. Brannan and his two companions had climbed the Sierra Nevadas, struggled across the wide deserts east of them, scaled the high peaks of the Wasatch Range, and walked to the famous Green

River Crossing on the Oregon Trail, covering eight hundred miles on foot. When they finally found Brigham and his camp, Brannan gave Brigham a rave review of California, citing all its many virtues: the warm climate, the ample rainfall, the rich soil, the lush vegetation, the plenitude of fish and game, and the fact that there would be no need for the great labor of installing an irrigation system, as there would be in the Great Salt Lake Valley.

Brannan did not understand Brigham's thinking at all. In describing California as a paradise, Brannan was only reinforcing Brigham's belief that California would be so desirable that it would attract too many non-Mormon settlers, who would inevitably come into conflict with the Saints.

In England and also on the Eastern Seaboard, Brigham had seen rapid expansion of the railroad. He knew that in a few short years rails would span the breadth of America. And in fact the final spike in the rail connecting the country from coast to coast was driven home in Utah, after a team of Mormon workers under Brigham's direction had smoothed and laid the roadbed, in 1869, within twenty-two years after Brigham's meeting with Brannan. Already in 1848, when that meeting took place, Brigham had witnessed the Oregon Trail crowded with wagon trains full of thousands of pioneers pushing on to the West Coast.

Brigham feared that when, inevitably in the near future, this mass settlement of California reached a population level that rendered the Mormons a minority, the pattern of persecution and violence that had been visited upon the Saints in Ohio, in Missouri, and in Illinois would reassert itself. Brigham sought isolation and independence, even at the price of harder living conditions. After joining the company on the remainder of their journey, Brannan traveled back to sunny California disappointed at his failure to change Brigham's mind.

Sticking to his original plans, Brigham led his company from the Green River crossing to Fort Bridger, the last outpost they would use on the Oregon Trail. Now would come the biggest challenge: from here to the Great Salt Lake Valley, the journey that lay before them was essentially untested trail. Shortly after pulling out of Fort Bridger, the Mormon wagon train veered onto a cutoff that eventually came to be known as the Hastings track. The entire path Brigham would now pioneer became known as the Mormon Trail.

All that existed of the trail when Brigham blazed it was the scarcely discernible remnants of the Donner Party's ill-fated passage along this southwesterly bias a year earlier. Members of the Donner Party had worked to clear a trail, but their work had been primitive and was now mostly overgrown. So going through the extremely challenging mountain terrain was rough. In addition to the faint traces of the Donner Party trail, Brigham had only primitive maps to guide him—and Orson Pratt, who had taught himself to use the sextant and plotted their course by the stars.

Then three days out of Fort Bridger an untoward thing happened. On July 12, Brigham came down with mountain fever. This common pioneer affliction had previously struck other members of the party, but when their guide and leader became a victim—and especially when Brigham became delirious—morale deteriorated. Anxiety had already been running high since the company pulled onto the Hastings Cutoff. Now the general apprehension rose even higher, as the company stayed put for three days while Brigham struggled with the fever.

After all, time was a crucial factor. This advance party had to reach the Great Salt Lake Valley and plant a crop in time to harvest it and feed the wagon trains full of Mormon pioneers moving along the trail behind them. Also, the advance party had to send a delegation back along the trail to guide those following parties before winter rendered parts of the trail impassable. The entire plan now seemed precarious. Morale was already low because of the harrowing terrain the party had to contend with, and all the members of Brigham's company had heard the reports

"This is the place"—the Great Salt Lake Valley.
Library of Congress

that the land they were headed for might not be able to produce crops.

At this point, Heber C. Kimball, Brigham's great friend and second in command, made an unorthodox but brilliant decision. Ignoring the conventional wisdom never to separate a wagon train, Kimball sent an advance party ahead to open the trail, under the direction of Orson Pratt and his sextant. At the same time, Wilford Woodruff fashioned a makeshift bed for Brigham in the back of his wagon, which he then positioned at the back of the train. As the main body of the wagons moved out, Woodruff, carrying Brigham, followed along behind at a steady but slower pace.

Six days later, on July 21, 1847, the first Mormons set foot in the Great Salt Lake Valley when Orson Pratt and Erastus Snow reached it together. The following day, the remainder of Brigham's company joined them. The next day, Orson Pratt and Brigham's cousin, Willard Richards, convened a prayer assembly and consecrated the land to God after giving thanks for the party's safe deliverance. And a day later, Brigham finally arrived, still bedridden in the back of Wilford Woodruff's wagon. Woodruff turned his wagon around once it had cleared the mouth of Emigration Canyon and drew up on the banks of Lake Bonneville. Lying in the back of the wagon, Brigham—like Moses seeing the Promised Land from the mountain—could behold the whole valley spread out below him. "This is the place," Brigham told Woodruff. He had seen it in a vision, and he knew this was the site for the ideal settlement the Saints had so long sought.

When Woodruff and Brigham reached the encampment at two that afternoon, Brigham was buoyed to see that the advance party had already plowed the earth, diverted a stream to irrigate the cultivated plot, and planted crops. But he could not afford to rest. Besides polling the pioneers to establish a consensus on the new site as a permanent settlement and then laying out a whole new city plan, Brigham also had to organize a party to return to Winter Quarters to guide and aid all the Saints still making the trek westward, and those about to set out. Having done much, he had much yet to do.

CHAPTER 19

BACKTRACKING TO WINTER QUARTERS

Despite intermittent recurrences of the agonies of mountain fever, Brigham got to work as soon and as hard as he could. Three days after arriving in the new Salt Lake Valley settlement with Woodruff, Brigham attended the general meeting convened to see if all the camp members were in agreement that this was the site on which to build the new Zion. Although Brigham was notoriously decisive and unflinching in the face of large responsibilities, he was not yet dictatorial. Therefore, he sought to establish full consent from the majority of the Saints on hand that this was the place where they would put down new and permanent roots. As it turned out, the decision in favor of the new location was all but unanimous. Only one Saint—William Vance—voted against it. He was overruled.

Then Brigham set to work creating a managerial hierarchy to apportion the new land and plan the city. The camp members elected the

Apostles to decide all issues in both areas. Almost immediately, Brigham, as the senior Apostle, set to work with his fellow Apostles to decide the size of city housing lots, how wide streets and sidewalks would be, what sections of the city would be zoned for business, and what animal control laws would obtain in the city. Most important, Brigham got agreement on the location and size of the temple lot. It was to be forty acres right in the center of the new city. Brigham chose a home site for himself and his family slightly to the east of the temple site, but handy to it.

After Brigham settled these civic policy issues, he preached a memorable sermon in which he explained what the settlement would stand for. First, the Saints would live in an atmosphere of total religious freedom with only one proviso: neither blasphemy of God nor any form of mockery of Joseph Smith would be tolerated. Other than that, people were entitled to worship as they chose. Second, the Saints would strive for complete self-sufficiency within their new Zion. They would be in no way dependent on non-Mormon communities to provide for their needs. They would manufacture, build, weave, spin, sew, or grow anything and everything they needed. They would establish every business necessary to achieve absolute self-reliance. Though this self-dependence was admirable in many respects, it did lead later to exclusionary business practices—favoritism and monopoly—that inhibited fair trade with outsiders.

Brigham spent a little over a month in the new settlement, putting his plans in action and also nursing himself back to what he hoped would be full health after the mountain fever. With the help of his administrative colleagues, mostly the Apostles and a few elders, during this period Brigham concentrated on making certain that the basic necessities for the new settlement were in place, at least on a temporary basis.

During this time he also managed to explore the surrounding area on horseback. Along with a few companions, Brigham rode to Ensign Peak and to the Great Salt Lake, where they all bathed, amazed at how buoyant the water was from its heavy deposits of salt. Brigham was disappointed that the lingering side effects of mountain fever recurred persistently all this while, causing him to lose precious working time. Despite this handicap, he pushed on as well as he could with the work to be done.

He wrote letters and dispensed advice the whole time. When the essentials for the new settlement were in place, some members of the advance party left ahead of Brigham himself to backtrack to Winter Quarters, retrieve their families, and start the westward journey anew. As these men departed the Salt Lake Valley, Brigham gave them letters to carry to other elders in charge of the wagon trains that already stretched out across Iowa and Nebraska. The letters contained encouragement and suggestions on how to proceed. Brigham also instructed the departing men to rein in their emotions when they reached Winter Quarters so that they would not unduly influence those yet to start the trip to embrace either too much optimism or too much pessimism.

One important letter he wrote was to the Mormon Battalion, then serving in California. In this letter, which he entrusted to Samuel Brannan for delivery, Brigham reached out to the Mormon troops to let them know of the new settlement and how keenly their arrival was desired. He encouraged them to come to the Salt Lake Valley and join the other Saints, knowing that their arrival would occasion celebration and great joy among those already settled there.

Brigham took another significant action before he headed back east to assist the wagon trains of Saints to follow: he baptized all the Apostles and then all the members of the advance pioneer company now settled in the valley. For the baptism, the Saints created a small pool of water by diverting and damming the Twin Creeks, which marked the borders of the planned new city. In this small pool of water, Brigham baptized everyone then in the encampment.

As the end of August drew near, Brigham decided that all was in order in the new settlement. He would now backtrack to Winter Quarters.

Before departing, he left specific instructions for the building of a sturdy stockade to enclose the new settlement in its entirety. He even specified the height of the stockade's walls. He wanted the new community as safe as possible from the incursions of wild animals and also from the possibility of attacks by forces hostile to the Mormons. In addition, Brigham spelled out the details of the homes to be constructed within the stockade while he was away.

Having accomplished all of this work in a matter of weeks, despite the setbacks to his health, Brigham mounted his horse on August 26 and rode out of the Great Salt Lake Valley through Emigration Canyon to a wagon train staging area at the Bear River. There he joined a company of slightly over a hundred men heading back to Winter Quarters to collect their families and lead them west to the new settlement. Five days later, the returning company broke camp at Bear River and set out eastward along the pioneering trail.

Within two days, Brigham's company met the first of four other companies of Saints strung out along the trail headed west. Over the next several days, Brigham's company passed all three other companies headed west. These four companies of Mormon pioneers would be the first to arrive in the Salt Lake Valley settlement after Brigham's advance company already there. A few weeks later, in September of 1847, these four companies arrived in the Salt Lake Valley. As Brigham met each new westward-bound company, he would stop and camp with them overnight, offering advice and suggestions, as well as encouragement, along with a description of the new venue that would soon be their future home.

One night, relaxed security led to a major mishap. Horse thieves rustled twenty-eight of the best horses Brigham's company had. With typical determination and unbreakable will, Brigham invited many of the men to join him on foot for the remaining seven-hundred-mile stretch of trail to Winter Quarters. Now forty-six years old, Brigham still had the vigor of the itinerant young preacher he had been in the 1830s, when he walked as many as two thousand miles a year traversing New York and New England making new converts. The men fell in step with Brigham and the returning company averaged an astonishing fifteen to twenty-five miles a day. They managed this daily distance despite the added burden on the remaining horses; the teams strained mightily while pulling the wagons, to the point where the men often had to help the exhausted horses to their feet in the morning. Fear grew that the horses would soon give out entirely.

Finally, Brigham ordered the company to leave the wagons and their teams at an encampment near the Platte River, in Iowa, to be retrieved later. Brigham had lightweight foodstuffs—mostly dried buffalo meat— prepared, and the company covered the last thirteen days of the journey on foot, hauling their own meals.

Brigham and company arrived back at Winter Quarters on October 26 with not one member lost and no real mishaps along the trail except for the theft of the horses and the strain this had placed on the company. All told, Brigham and the returning members of his advance party had been gone for over six months and had traveled more than two thousand miles round-trip. But they had found the promised land they had so long sought.

CHAPTER 20

EXODUS

COMPLETED

Even though the settlement was in place in the Salt Lake Valley, Brigham still had big challenges to confront. One was administrative. After nearly three years at the helm of the church only by virtue of being the senior Apostle, Brigham realized that the office of the First Presidency—an office in abeyance since the murder of Joseph Smith—needed to be reinstated. The Twelve Apostles were too difficult to gather for councils and quorums—scattered afar serving their primary function: preaching the new gospel and gathering converts. As the preeminent member of the new First Presidency, Brigham would be able to head up a more nimble executive oversight group. Therefore, back at Winter Quarters in December of 1847, Brigham reinstituted the office of the First Presidency and was duly elected the new president by the Quorum of Twelve. Brigham then chose Heber Chase Kimball as first counselor and Willard Richards as second counselor; together Brigham, Kimball, and Richards made up the reinstituted First Presidency, with Brigham at its head. Brigham also realized he had to address the vacancies among the Apostles, but he put that obligation off temporarily to focus his attention on the problems of the exodus.

The federal government had requested that the Mormons remove their Winter Quarters settlement from the Nebraska side of the Missouri River back to the Iowa side. Federal officials had made this request for a shift back to the east bank of the river because the Omaha tribe, on whose lands in Florence, Nebraska, Winter Quarters encroached, had grown restive and disenchanted with the Mormon visitors and their consumption of land, game, fowl, and fish. Brigham felt that the federal government had again disappointed the Saints, but as he had always done, he chose to avoid potential conflict. So during the winter of 1847–1848, Brigham supervised the transfer of the Mormon settlement to Council Bluffs, Iowa, from Florence, Nebraska.

He chose to emphasize the positive. In December, he and the Apostles issued a general letter to all Mormons worldwide. This letter first reported how the exodus had proceeded so far, and then it gave an update on the reconstituted First Presidency, urged faith and devotion to the tenets of the church, and encouraged all Saints to gather in the Great Salt Lake Valley. It also requested that any tract on education the Saints could obtain be forwarded to church headquarters or brought along personally to the new settlement. As always, the Saints were urged to educate their children. In view of Brigham's intention to make the desert bloom, the letter also requested all pilgrims to the Salt Lake Valley to bring every kind of choice seeds they could obtain, whether for grain or vegetables, fruit or shrubs, trees or vines. The same directive held for livestock and tools. The best poultry and farm animals were to be brought along, as were the best tools for any and every job.

Brigham always sought to optimize the useful potential of all converts. He knew that many converts were oppressed in poverty in England and in other parts of Europe, and he wanted them to bring their skills and tools and use them to flourish in egalitarian America, both to their personal benefit and to the benefit of the always resourceful and industrious Mormons collectively. In this regard, Brigham set the example, utilizing all of his agricultural and building skills to maximum effect whenever needed, as he had recently demonstrated in leading the construction of the large raft at the final Platte River crossing with the advance company.

Brigham also needed to evoke the highest level of commitment possible from the huge contingents of Saints about to make the journey from Winter Quarters to the Great Salt Lake Valley beginning in the spring. Brigham fully realized that this journey would be the most difficult yet. Instead of taking small parties of experienced pioneers and skilled craftsmen across the rough terrain of the plains and the mountains, Brigham would now be leading a multitude of inexperienced pioneers, many of them women and children. Nearly all of the newer emigrants had never traversed rough wilderness, and few of them had the skills of the able-bodied young men who had blazed the trail with the advance party the previous year.

To make the long and difficult migration possible, Brigham elected to break the huge wagon train into three companies. Each company would be under the direction of a member of the First Presidency. Brigham would lead the first company and Heber Kimball the second. These two companies would meet at the designated staging area on the Elkhorn River. In combination, the two companies were most likely the largest wagon train ever to traverse the Oregon Trail and the Mormon Trail. According to Francis M. Gibbons's *Brigham Young: Modern Moses, Prophet of God*, the two companies totaled 623 wagons and

1,891 emigrants; and they took 2,012 oxen, 131 horses, forty-four mules, 983 cows, 334 loose cattle, 654 sheep, 237 pigs, 904 chickens, 134 dogs, 54 cats, 3 goats, 10 geese, 11 doves, 5 ducks, and a lone squirrel along with them. There were also 5 beehives on the wagons to ensure that the new promised land had honey as well as milk.

At first the trip was jovial and inspired, just as it had been for the advance party, with the musicians in the wagon train playing lively tunes at night for recreational singing and dancing. But as the trail became harder, anxiety set in. The dusty passage across the pest-infested Badlands did not help, nor did the horrible terrain in the mountains. Morale sank.

By the time the wagon train reached the Sweetwater River in what is today western Wyoming, the grumbling was general. Brigham did not resort to another tongue-lashing—such as he had given to the advance company the previous year—probably because he sensed that only an extreme gesture would motivate them. So he made one. First he invited all who were willing to follow him to do so, then he took his wagon and rode off over the horizon. Amid shock and more grumbling, the huge wagon train followed.

A few weeks earlier, Brigham had made a smart strategic move. Two days past Chimney Rock, the famous landmark at roughly the midway point of the journey, he had sent couriers on horseback ahead with letters for Parley P. Pratt and John Taylor, two Apostles who had remained at the new settlement in the Great Salt Lake Valley, requesting that they send a train of wagons to rendezvous at the Green River crossing with Brigham's huge wagon train headed their way. One of the relief wagons coming from the new settlement was to carry a load of salt for the animals in Brigham's enormous company.

It turned out that the relief train rendezvoused with Brigham's encampment early, east of the Green River crossing. Led by Abraham O. Smoot and Brigham's brother Lorenzo Dow Young, the relief contingent

converged with Brigham's company on August 28 at the last crossing of
the Sweetwater. Using great foresight, Lorenzo and Abraham brought
along forty-seven empty wagons and, even more helpful, 124 additional
yoke of oxen to aid the pioneers in scaling the steep mountain passes at
the end of the trail, beyond which nestled the Great Salt Lake Valley.
Brigham was also able to dispatch a good number of these empty wagons back to Winter Quarters for use by future companies of Mormon
emigrants heading west the following spring.

Lorenzo and Abraham also brought great news. The new settlement
in the Great Salt Lake Valley had managed to reap a good harvest that
would more than supply the nutritional needs of all the many new
emigrants soon to arrive there. This news was no doubt a great relief to
Brigham. Jim Bridger's dire warnings about the impossibility of growing
grain and other crops in the arid soil of this area of the Great Basin must
have haunted Brigham—and his worries would only have been increased
when snow fell early on September 14 as the long wagon train forded
the Bear River, only a short distance from their destination.

Brigham also knew that the settlement back at Winter Quarters had
reaped a good harvest the previous autumn and had no doubt repeated
the feat this year, meaning that Saints at both ends of the trail would be
well nourished. This boded well for future wagon trains starting the long
trek from Winter Quarters.

Six days after the early snowfall at Bear River, Brigham topped Big
Mountain on September 20 and saw below him in the distance the Great
Salt Lake Valley spread out in all its natural beauty. In good health and
fine spirits this time, unhampered by mountain fever, he descended once
again through the winding Emigration Canyon, ready to undertake the
enormous role of prime mover in building the ideal community the
Saints would construct with unflinching determination and grit, in an
amazingly short period of time.

CHAPTER 21

THE COLONIZER

ight from the start, Brigham Young had his work cut out for him in the Great Salt Lake Valley. His influence as a colonizer of the American West arguably exceeds that of any other individual. When Brigham was rejoicing to learn that the advance pioneering party had managed to reap a good harvest that autumn of 1848, he could not have foreseen the brutal challenge the winter of 1848–1849 would visit upon him and the other settlers. With the arrival of Willard Richards's third company in the valley, the number of Mormon pioneers there exceeded two thousand five hundred souls. Shelter was the first necessity; everyone had to be established on a plot of land. This Brigham did by granting "inheritances"; earlier he had decreed that no one could purchase land in the settlement.

In planning the community, Brigham once again harked back to practices he had learned from Joseph Smith. He divided the city with

wide streets and instituted zoning to sequester the business and industrial districts from the residential areas. He apportioned land to settlers
according to their needs. Some would receive larger plots more distant
from the town center to be used for farming; others would receive
smaller and more central plots for town living. Brigham sectioned off a
church farm of eight hundred acres dedicated to aiding the entire community.

Building codes applied throughout the city. Most of the early structures would be made of mud, so adobe yards appeared. A canal provided
water for home use and allowed for agricultural irrigation. Brigham
ordered a wall built around the central forty acres on which the temple
would be constructed. He also directed the construction of a clerk's office
and of a council house. Fortunately, many homes and other buildings
were completed before the heavy snow fell that winter, beginning in early
December. The eventual accumulation of five feet of snow forced the
pioneers to dig in and await the arrival of spring before they could
resume construction.

The severe cold and the tremendous snowfall induced a great deal
of stress among the settlers. Carping and complaining broke out again,
and Brigham had to use all his powers of encouragement and persuasion
to tamp down talk of pushing west to California with its milder climate
and its ready-made agricultural advantages. He also had to dissuade
some settlers from planning to move back east in the spring, using vivid
words to evoke powerful memories of the abuse and violence, the political bias and social exclusion imposed on Mormons in the states back
east.

With the arrival of spring, the pioneers perked up and, heedful of
Brigham's endorsement of the Great Salt Lake Valley as the place to put
down permanent roots, went on a building spree spanning the spring,
summer, and fall of 1849. Besides constructing a bridge across the Jordan
River to the west, they built several bridges across smaller streams and

creeks in the vicinity. In addition, they erected three grist mills, six or seven saw mills, and a community bathhouse at the warm springs. All of this construction pleased Brigham enormously and his enthusiasm, as always, proved contagious.

Brigham soon had to turn his attention again to issues of governance, both church and secular. On February 12, he ordained four Apostles to fill the vacancies that had been created by the excommunications resulting from the leadership crisis in the wake of the Smith assassination and by promotions to the First Presidency. Franklin D. Richards, Charles C. Rich, who had been so helpful on the drive west, and the Snow brothers, Erastus and Lorenzo, became Apostles. With the Quorum of the Twelve Apostles restored to full strength and with the reinstitution of the First Presidency, Brigham had restored the ecclesiastical hierarchy to its original strength under Joseph Smith. He was now at the apex of a strong church government.

Secular government was a trickier issue. When the advance company had arrived in the previous summer of 1847, the Great Salt Lake Valley where the Mormons had settled still belonged to Mexico. The following year, with the end of the Mexican-American War, the Treaty of Guadalupe Hidalgo ceded vast tracts of land to the United States, including many tracts of land that today constitute large segments of the Far West and Southwest, including the Mormon settlement in the Great Salt Lake Valley. That meant the Mormons were now technically under United States jurisdiction, but there existed no means of communication by which such jurisdiction could be exercised. The new Mormon settlement was simply too far into the wilderness for Washington to control.

Therefore Brigham exercised the Mormon self-government that he had for so many years dreamed of and sought to attain. By way of possession of the land he claimed ownership. He correctly believed that the United States government would, in time, assert its federal authority, but in the meantime he claimed ownership of the land and simply extended the ecclesiastical governance of the church to include civil matters for the new city, called Salt Lake City, and the communities that surrounded it.

This extension of ecclesiastical governance over civil matters would cause problems right from the start. In the beginning these problems were minor, but over the years, as the non-Mormon population grew, they became large and severe. In time these problems would cause Brigham's power to unravel—when he radically overstepped the bounds of his legitimate authority and became despotic to Utah's citizens and rebellious against the federal government and its appointed officials and judges.

But in these early days, Brigham made allowances for non-Mormon outsiders and took measures to make them feel that his government would be fair and impartial. Ever mindful of past violence against Mormons that had arisen when non-Mormons felt potentially disenfranchised by Mormons, he knew that there would shortly be an influx of non-Mormon settlers to the entire Great Basin, an area roughly the size of Texas. The Great Basin, after all, of which the Great Salt Lake Valley was only a small part, extended from the Rockies in the east to the Sierra Nevadas in the west, from the Columbia River watershed in the north to the Grand Canyon in the south. It encompassed all or parts of nine of our present-day states. And the influx of non-Mormons would eventually result in a vast non-Mormon population living side by side with the large Mormon population, which numbered twenty thousand by the early 1850s.

Fully realizing that this vast region could not be openly and solely governed by the Mormon priesthood—however much that was exactly what he wanted in his heart—in March of 1849, Brigham issued a constitution for what he called the Territory of Deseret. He was promptly elected governor. Deseret, incidentally, is a word used in *The Book of Mormon*; it means "honeybee." It is wholly appropriate that Utah eventually gained the nickname "The Beehive State."

To this day, many Mormons believe that Brigham and his colleagues in church governance at the time made a strategic mistake in requesting that the federal government create a territorial government for Deseret. These dissenting Mormons believe that the Saints should have immediately sought statehood, not recognition as a territory. But this is cloudy thinking. It is highly unlikely that statehood would have been granted to so vast a region when its population numbered only twelve thousand: at that time, statehood typically required a population five times higher. Plus, the lingering suspicion of Mormons among non-Mormons, especially when it came to political and judicial power, formed an additional obstacle to statehood. What's more, a great deal of repugnance over the practice of polygamy already existed among non-Mormons, even though the church would not publicly acknowledge this practice until 1852.

From March of 1849 until September of 1850, the provisional Territory of Deseret existed under the governorship of Brigham Young. During that time, the second anniversary of the advent of Mormons in the Great Basin in July of 1849 sparked an elaborate celebration. An oversized flag sewn by two of Brigham's plural wives bore the blue and white colors of Deseret, martial music was accompanied by cannon fire, and there was a processional of elders that amounted to a parade. On the one hand, Mormons were excited about their independence, but they also wanted to be part of the United States. Their ambivalence crystallized in Brigham Young's inciting the large crowd to cheer a public reading of the Declaration of Independence.

Brigham meant the declaration to apply mainly to the new nation of Deseret, and yet having it read aloud also stirred up feelings of loyalty to the United States. This one-foot-in-one-foot-out attitude pretty much summed up the paradoxical nature of Mormons' self-governance and their attitude toward the larger nation at the time. Bear in mind that loyalties in tension—a union versus a confederacy, centralized governance versus states' rights—constituted a profound American problem that dated back to the Constitutional Convention in 1787. Beginning at least at that time, this debate never went away—and seventy-four years later, in 1861, it erupted into the Civil War. And even that war did not finally resolve the related debate between big government and small government. That debate rages on even today.

The next important event in the Mormon governance saga occurred on September 9, 1850, when Congress passed an act reducing the Territory of Deseret and renaming it the Territory of Utah. At the same time, Congress created in addition the New Mexico Territory, which included what are now the states of New Mexico and Arizona. The Utah Territory covered what today includes the states of Utah and Nevada, with sections of Colorado and Wyoming thrown in.

Eleven days later, President Millard Fillmore appointed Brigham Young the Utah Territory's first governor, a position he would hold for just under eight years. Brigham considered his appointment vindication for his claims of Mormon "theodemocracy" as Joseph Smith had deemed the type of government the Mormons desired. And during Brigham's time as territorial governor, the Mormons were indeed exempt from the bias and violence they had suffered back in Ohio, Missouri, and Illinois. But their wish for ecclesiastical rule was at odds with the United States Constitution.

Separation of church and state amounted to a cornerstone of American governance. The Saints' virtual theocracy was on a collision course with the will of the American people to keep religion and government separate. As more non-Mormons settled in the Utah Territory, the Mormons would be forced to face the reality that no theocracy would be allowed to thrive on American soil.

The final showdown would not take place until eight years later, when Brigham, grown despotic, pressed for de facto Mormon autonomy—and then defied the federal government in his attempt to secure it. But in the immediate aftermath of Brigham's federal appointment as territorial governor, the Mormons flourished. With his usual foresight, Brigham had already divided and subdivided the original settlement and dispatched colonizing teams to set up communities similar to Salt Lake City in the surrounding regions. As early as 1847, right after the Mormons arrived in the West, Brigham had sent parties of 150 seasoned settlers to establish new communities mostly in the nearby valleys.

Then, in late 1849, Brigham had ratcheted up this colonizing effort, organizing an exploratory party under the leadership of Apostle Parley P. Pratt to search what amounted to the whole territory for new sites for settlements. The party left Salt Lake City in November and swept through the territory in a large circle. Also toward the end of 1849, another, smaller party left Salt Lake City with a guide and traveled to California. A few years later, still skeptical about the suitability of California for Mormons, Brigham reluctantly acceded to the wishes of others and approved the establishment of a Mormon settlement in

The Beehive House. *AdStock RF / Shutterstock.com*

San Bernardino. He also saw to it that Mormon communities sprouted along what came to be called "the Mormon Corridor" that passes through southern Utah and Nevada along the way to San Bernardino.

While handling all of these administrative and executive duties, Brigham still found time to settle his family into large quarters in Salt Lake City. By now he had thirteen wives and eighteen children, some of whom had grown up and left his household. His two oldest daughters, Elizabeth and Vilate, had married and moved out. That still left him with nearly thirty mouths to feed, and he energetically attended to his responsibilities as a patriarch, considering his duty to feed, shelter, and care for all members of his family his first responsibility, more worthy of his energy and efforts than anything else in his life.

Within a few short years, Brigham would build the Lion House and the Beehive House for his large family, but until then all family members had to shift with the smaller adobe structures he could provide. Polygamy was one of Brigham's two blind spots—the other being Mormon theocracy. In the coming years, the Saints would need to relinquish both these features of their religion and lifestyle before the acceptance of Mormons as full United States citizens would be achieved. Utah failed to achieve statehood for decades until polygamy was officially outlawed within the Utah Territory in 1890, when church president Wilford Woodruff announced that the church would obey federal anti-polygamy laws. But in his lifetime, Brigham never fully or truly accommodated himself to either of the bedrock American principles of monogamy and separation of church and state.

In the early days of settlement in Salt Lake City and in his own early years as territorial governor, Brigham concentrated not only on his domestic responsibilities but also on his obligation to proselytize for the new church, just as he had in his youthful days as a missionary and more recently as an Apostle. At a general conference held in October 1849, he had shocked his fellow Apostles by announcing new and far-flung assignments for them as missionaries. He dispatched some to Italy, France, Germany, and Scandinavia, in addition to sending others to help Orson Pratt, already in place in England. Considering missionary work as a church essential, a high priority, Brigham always pushed aggressively to ensure that it was carried out thoroughly and enthusiastically.

Because Brigham had witnessed firsthand how many downtrodden and abused people in England had embraced the new faith and emigrated to America, he set up a system in September of 1850 whereby the expenses of traveling to America could be provided in advance as long as restitution to the church was made when the new emigrants were in place in America and on a more secure economic footing. This system of aid became known as the Perpetual Emigration Fund Company. It lasted for four decades and enabled converts from all over the world to embrace the new faith and emigrate successfully to America. The fund operated on a restitution principle very similar to later federal programs such as the G.I. Bill and federal student loans for college tuition. Creating the fund enabled Brigham to fulfill his dream to see a stream of converts populating the mountains and valleys of Deseret with Latter-day Saints.

Brigham's colonizing vision of building ideal Mormon communities in the Western desert quickly turned to fact. In the two decades following his second arrival in Salt Lake City in 1848, when he took up permanent residence there, seventy thousand Mormon converts arrived by way of the Mormon Trail. Almost all of them quickly settled into the new communities—and their descendants still live there today.

CHAPTER 22

THE GOVERNOR

he realization of Brigham's dream of living in an isolated desert paradise totally self-governed and free from outside authority or interference was short-lived. A few weeks after President Fillmore appointed Brigham governor, the president dispatched a cadre of federal judges and other territorial officials to Utah. These men came west to set up various territorial administrative departments they deemed to be beyond Brigham's authority. Brigham did not share this view, and friction and jockeying for position broke out.

The tenures of this first wave of officials were short. Understandably, they came with the preconceived notion that they were in charge, in accordance with their federal appointments. They did not factor in Mormon intransigence. They did not expect to be undermined and rejected by Mormon elders—and by Governor Brigham Young himself, usually working behind the scenes. The Mormons wanted self-rule, and worse, they wanted ecclesiastical self-rule, expressly forbidden by the United States constitution. Given the Mormon suspicions of outside authority, it is not surprising that the original group of federally appointed territorial officials had to be quickly withdrawn to Washington. Once settled back in Washington these shocked and rejected officials told their side of the story about the strife in Utah, blaming it on Mormon intransigence bordering on open rebellion, with the Mormon church leaders back-channeling to their followers the message that insubordination was appropriate since Mormons should be governed according to the law of God as interpreted by their Mormon priests, Apostles, and elders, instead of by any outside secular authority.

The Mormons, on the other hand, contended that these first federal appointees had arrived in Utah with prejudices against the Mormons and then proceeded to wield too heavy a judicial and administrative hand. The view of Mormonism held by these federal officials, based as it was on over two decades of rumors interspersed with some facts, was somewhat exaggerated. Once again, and seemingly as always, the issue of plural marriage proved a difficult hurdle for these outsiders to take in stride. It was a lightning rod for prejudice and for all sorts of misgivings about what kind of people the Saints were.

When these first federal appointees arrived in August of 1850, Brigham welcomed them and introduced them to the church hierarchy. He also made them comfortable and took pains to ensure that they had the best accommodations available even though local accommodations were primitive compared to what they were used to back east. Among the first appointees to arrive was Judge Perry E. Brocchus, a man driven by ambition and not above political maneuvering to achieve personal power and material gains. After looking things over for a few weeks, he asked Brigham if he might address a general assembly of Latter-day Saints. Brigham acceded to his wish.

Brocchus proceeded to lay a gigantic egg. He mounted the speaker's platform on the Bowery, right on Temple Square, and spoke for two hours, addressing subjects a more sensitive and prudent man would never have broached. After thanking the Saints for the lavish concern and care they had shown him when he fell ill shortly after arriving, Brocchus jumped right into a discussion of theology and polygamy. He also defended the hands-off role the federal government had played during the Mormon persecutions in Missouri and Illinois—something the Saints had good reason to resent as a travesty of justice, considering how President Martin Van Buren had effectively washed his hands of the Mormons, failing to provide protection for them on the grounds that such matters had to be settled locally within the states. But local state authorities or those in league with them were the ones persecuting the Mormons with their state militias in the first place.

Brocchus's insensitive remarks and accusations led to murmurs and stirrings of disapproval in the audience, especially when he cast aspersions on what he characterized as a Mormon lack of patriotism. To make matters worse, he then begun talking about the role of virtuous women in civilized society, asserting that the Mormon practice of polygamy was inconsistent with virtue in women. This was too much for the audience to bear.

More important, it was too much for Brigham to bear. He rose and rebutted the judge forcefully, accusing him of being either ignorant or wicked, or both. By this time, Brigham was a polished rhetorician. He persuasively argued the Mormon case that the federal government had failed to protect them and had, in effect, sanctioned the depredations visited upon them in Missouri and later in Illinois. Brigham stated firmly that the do-nothing federal authorities had the blood of dead Mormon women and children on their hands.

Upping the ante, Brigham then addressed the issue of Brocchus's insulting attacks on Mormon doctrine and on Mormon marital practices.

He pointed out that most federal officials were egregiously corrupt and on the make and that they had some nerve to question or impugn the virtue of any Saints, let alone the women. To insinuate that Mormons were in any way collectively lax in morals or virtue was an outrageous insult to the entire community.

After this inauspicious debut by Judge Brocchus, it is not surprising that he lasted less than three full weeks before President Fillmore had to recall him to Washington. Along with Brocchus, Chief Justice Lemuel H. Brandebury, territorial secretary Broughton D. Harris, and sub-Indian agent Henry R. Day also had to retreat back east hastily. A tragicomic element marked their exit, at least in the Mormon telling of the story. The three tried to pass last-minute legislation that would have permitted them not to relinquish the territorial funds to the U.S. marshal in charge—in other words, the departing trio was seeking to abscond with the loot. The Mormons accused other officials of being on the take as well, and rumors circulated that Brocchus was a drunkard. There were other corrupt federal appointees and officials in the Utah Territory, mostly connected with army administration or with the administration of what was then called Indian Affairs.

The federal officials defended their honesty and justified denying the federal funds to the Mormons on the grounds that the Mormons were wholly insubordinate to the point of open rebellion. Nevertheless, the Mormons dubbed this incident the tale of the "run-away officers." Mormons in general viewed it as a victory. So, too, did Brigham Young, who felt that his clout in Washington, long nurtured by Mormon lobbyists, had now firmly secured him the upper hand in governing the Utah Territory. This mistaken assumption would embolden him in the coming years, encourage him to overstep the bounds of his gubernatorial authority, and eventually result in his removal as governor.

But in the near term, Brigham's intercession in the nation's capital by way of Mormon emissaries and friends carried the day: this initial group of federal officials was replaced by more malleable men who were less imbued, according to the Mormons way of thinking, with anti-Mormon prejudice and less inclined to line their pockets and to embrace unattractive personal habits. For nearly eight years, Brigham was able to work with the replacement federal officials, while preserving large administrative and judicial roles for himself and other high-ranking church officials. In plain words, despite constant friction and outbreaks of strife, church and state jurisdictions remained at least nominally separate, but in reality Brigham Young retained the final say.

During Brigham's nearly eight years administering the Utah Territory as governor, he managed to set an agenda that would serve as a template for Mormon life then and thereafter. When gold appeared at Sutter's Mill in northern California and set off the gold rush, Brigham guided his people well in coping with the subsequent hysteria. The Mormons shortly had to handle an influx of prospectors intent on reaching the California gold fields, but, like the ill-fated Donner Party, many of these prospectors arrived too late in their transcontinental crossing to brave the Sierra Nevadas in autumn. Most of these prospectors came by wagon trains using the Hastings Cutoff and traversing the Mormon Trail. And once stranded by the onset of winter, these stragglers, many of them shiftless prospectors, settled temporarily in Salt Lake City, the biggest town between St. Louis and San Francisco. For the years of the gold rush, Brigham and the Mormons mainly shared their foodstuffs and shelter with these stranded prospectors and extended them other forms of hospitality, though friction sometimes occurred.

The flow of pioneers and prospectors through Salt Lake City had a good effect: it spurred local commerce. But it also had a countervailing bad effect: Brigham was forced to counsel his people not to contract gold fever and rush off to balmy California in search of an easy life and fortune, but instead to stick to their life in the harsher mountain clime of Utah, which was much healthier spiritually. Throughout the years of this get-rich-quick threat, Brigham held his community together with admirable steadiness. And he was ever the wily businessman. When Mormons did strike gold or any other rich mineral deposit, Brigham quickly counseled tithing and often moved in to set up a larger operation to exploit the source of revenue to the maximum. And Brigham often had a financial interest in the larger operation he put in place.

In the exact same sure-handed way, Brigham managed over the years of his governorship to tamp down most internal or theological dissension and to avoid the crippling controversies that had divided the church first in Kirtland and then in Nauvoo, especially during the months of contention for the leadership of the Saints following the murder of Joseph Smith. During these early years in Utah, Brigham applied his considerable diplomacy to maintain church harmony, with only a few minor exceptions. Also, even as Mormon isolation was diminishing with so many non-Mormon pioneers moving into the territory, Brigham mostly avoided the violence that had marred Mormon life back east.

Brigham set yet another precedent in the way he handled the question of integration with the Native Americans. At first he was enlightened and tolerant, deeming them savages who stole to survive and had no concept that they were doing anything unethical, immoral, or illegal. But in January of 1850, he authorized a war against the Utes after they kept disrupting Mormon settlers, sometimes wounding or even killing them, and often rustling the settlers' livestock. Brigham and the Mormon settlers justified their killing of the Utes—not so different from many incidents in the U.S. Army's dismal record of mistreating and exterminating the Indians—because God had led the Mormons to their desert Zion. The Mormons simply considered taking control of this land their manifest destiny. The Native Americans, of course, were acting out against the Mormons in retaliation for the usurpation of their hunting and fishing grounds and the resulting food shortage. This was the Native American motive for rustling livestock, especially cattle, to butcher and eat.

In the January 1850 instance of Mormon aggression against the Utes, Brigham gave in to pressure from settlers in and near what is now Provo. He sanctioned raids against the Utes and an atrocity resulted. Eleven unarmed warriors, after being assured of safety if they surrendered and disarmed, were summarily executed. This pattern of Mormon assurances followed by wholesale execution would appear again years later in the worst moment in Brigham Young's history and in that of the Mormons: the Mountain Meadows Massacre, described in detail in a later chapter. The 1850 campaign against the Utes and other tribes continued until the fall of that year, with dozens more Native Americans killed. The result was Mormon appropriation of the Utah Valley.

In the years following the 1850 Mormon campaign against the Native Americans, as ensuing disputes erupted over access to land, game, livestock, and grazing rights, incidents and atrocities on both sides flared up. One of the worst occurred in the summer of 1853, when the Walker War broke out between the Mormon settlers and the tribe of Chief Walker, whom Brigham had befriended and helped from the earliest years of Mormon settlement in the Great Salt Lake Valley. When the bloodshed threatened to get completely out of hand, Brigham took action, at considerable personal risk, visiting the chief in his tepee. Employing all of his negotiating and diplomatic skills, Brigham defused a potentially violent situation and arrived at a peace agreement acceptable to both parties. At the end of negotiations, Brigham sat in a tribal counsel and smoked a calumet to honor the peace settlement.

Unfortunately, this peaceful settlement would prove more the exception than the norm, even though Brigham Young tried to be benevolent. But like most nineteenth-century Americans, Young and the Mormons regarded Native Americans and African Americans with patriarchal disdain. Members of both groups could not attain full membership or first-class citizenship within the Mormon faith. The two worst stains on American domestic policy are the genocide of the Native Americans and the peculiar institution in which African Americans were enslaved. The Mormons are not alone in putting their own stamp on the abuse and slaughter of Native Americans, and it is disappointing that the Utah and New Mexico territories permitted slavery at a time when outlawing it was more prevalent in federal territories hoping for statehood.

To digress a moment, recall that back in 1820 the very question of free versus slave states had led to the Missouri Compromise, but the net result forty-one years later was the worst calamity in American history, the Civil War. During the forty intervening years between the Missouri Compromise and the outbreak of the Civil War, the Mormons, going by *The Book of Mormon*, considered Native Americans a lost tribe called the Lamanites, who, according to Joseph Smith, sometimes had to be killed; the Mormons also adhered to the prevailing nineteenth-century view that, according to the Bible, black people were "marked" or "cursed" by God, like Cain and his descendents for the murder of Abel, or like Ham and his offspring because Ham had seen his father Noah naked. Absurd as these views appear now, back then they held sway. In fact, until fairly recent times, blacks and Native Americans, though allowed to be Mormons, were not extended the full privileges of church membership accorded to whites.

On a brighter note, Brigham, while governor, delivered on his promise to make the Saints in Utah self-sufficient. Besides all the normal building and agricultural businesses that every burgeoning Western settlement sprouted, Brigham drew upon his knowledge of blacksmithing to start an iron works. His blacksmithing skills did not fully match the task of starting an iron foundry, but this proved no deterrent to the project. Brigham always thought he could attract emigrants and pioneers with the necessary knowledge, and over time he did set up an iron foundry in this way. He also drew upon his elementary knowledge of tanning to attract followers with the requisite knowledge to set up a booming tannery. Over the years of his administration, Brigham also expanded Mormon retailing operations; he exploited the gold rush crowds and the flow of pioneers passing through Salt Lake City by helping fellow Mormons establish a great many retail shops and outlets vending goods imported from back East. As a thriving commercial nexus between St. Louis and San Francisco, Salt Lake City boomed.

Another part of Brigham Young's legacy as governor will redound to his glory forever. As he had preached for years, he prized education to the highest degree. Thus Brigham and the

Brigham Young. *Library of Congress*

Mormons, following Joseph Smith's precedent, had always set up schools. Joseph Smith had established a school and a seminary as far back as Kirtland. Even in the early days in Ohio, the Saints imported scholars to lecture and teach. Later, Brigham was especially proud that in their foreign missionary work the Saints were able, through education, to raise the English poor, the dregs of the Industrial Revolution, to the level of basic literacy and numeracy.

As governor, Brigham, a man with only those eleven days of formal schooling, first set up an elementary educational system for the whole community in the Utah Territory. Then he founded the University of Deseret in Salt Lake City on February 28, 1850. Today it is known as the University of Utah and is highly respected in academic circles. Not only that; the University of Deseret split and spawned another formidable educational institution, Brigham Young University in Provo, just forty miles south of Salt Lake City in the shadow of the Wasatch Range.

Because vilification of the Mormons continued in the press during Brigham's time as governor, he stepped up the application of publicity and public relations lessons learned from Joseph Smith in Kirtland and in Nauvoo. Brigham founded several newspapers around the country, most notably in New York City and in St. Louis. These Mormon newspapers promulgated the news as the Mormons perceived it; the papers also disseminated Mormon doctrine and gospel. Brigham sought especially to give Mormons a countervailing voice wherever and whenever slander and calumny of Mormons took the form of wild and unfounded rumors, something the Saints had to tolerate for more than two and a half decades before Brigham managed to establish an alternative voice in the national press.

Another part of Brigham's legacy was the building of the new Temple in Salt Lake City, though he didn't live to see the completion of this great edifice, which still stands in the center of Temple Square in Salt Lake City today. But he did set up the Mormon Tabernacle Choir that is world famous for performing there. Brigham also set up temples in the surrounding Mormon communities in the Utah Territory, overseeing their construction and their internal decoration in minute detail, with the discerning eye of the former building contractor. He was especially proud of the temple he built in St. George, the spa-like southern Utah community where Brigham and his family often vacationed in winter.

During his governorship, Brigham made one great mistake as a colonizer. The famous debacle of the two thousand handcart pioneers in 1856 shows Mormon grit at its best, but it also illustrates foolhardiness on the part of Mormon leaders, including Brigham. Because money was tight, Brigham wanted to use cheaper handcarts instead of expensive wagons for converts making the trek to Utah over the Mormon Trail from Iowa. Four companies using handcarts made the trip in 1856, two leaving in June and arriving in late September and early October, their members hungry and tired but mostly safe and sound. Two others, the Willie Company and the Martin Company, named for their respective leaders, James Willie and Edward Martin, consisting almost entirely of emigrants from England, left too late, in high summer, and got trapped in severe autumn weather and heavy snowfalls in the mountains.

Brigham and the elders sent relief wagons, but between the two companies over two hundred emigrants, or one in ten, perished. Brigham blamed others, shifting responsibility away from himself and onto them. But clearly he had misjudged the ability of the emigrants to withstand the deprivation and pain he had withstood traveling by foot as a young preacher and as a member of Zion's Camp in 1834 in Missouri. Moreover, back then he wasn't traveling in the high Rockies in winter conditions. He had made a tragic mistake and would soon make a worse one the following year.

Yet practically everything admirable the Mormons stand for today— and that amounts to a great deal—can be traced back to Brigham's leadership, especially during the heroic years of the exodus and the early years of his governorship. That is all the more reason to regret that Brigham's reign as governor ended on a sour note.

In early 1857, the newly installed president, James Buchanan, not a man celebrated for his measured judgment, overreacted to reports of Mormon intransigence and non-cooperation with the federal territorial authorities. When Brigham in response overreacted to Buchanan's impetuosity and foolhardiness, the result was the completely avoidable and somewhat farcical Utah War, also known to history as "Buchanan's Blunder." Yet it was tragic, too, because of the useless bloodletting. The Utah War, in bringing out Brigham's tendencies to despotism and ruth- lessness, proved to be his darkest moment—and the beginning of his downfall.

CHAPTER 23

THE UTAH WAR

B esides also being known to history as "Buchanan's Blunder," the Utah War goes by several other names as well: the Utah Expedition, the Utah Campaign, the Mormon War, and the Mormon Rebellion. It should never have happened. Buchanan deserves the opprobrium heaped on him for his "blunder." Brigham's judgment faltered here, too; however, given the history of Mormon persecution and abuse, Brigham's error in overreacting to the president's impetuous stupidity is easier to understand—though, given the results, possibly not easier to forgive.

Every dispute has three sides: one each for the disputants, and then the truth of the matter. That truth is often hard to determine. Still, it's clear President Buchanan was behaving recklessly when he dispatched twenty-five hundred federal troops to Utah to bring Brigham Young and his Mormon followers into line. What incited the president to take this drastic and ill-considered action was the dissatisfaction of federal territorial officials in 1857 with what they deemed to be Brigham's heavy-handed interference within their jurisdiction.

As always, Brigham had attempted to put ecclesiastical authority over secular authority. He honored the rule of God and not the rule of man. Brigham's authority constantly overshadowed that of the federal officials assigned to govern the Utah Territory, and they maintained that Brigham's power ran counter to the federal constitution's separation of church and state. They claimed that he constantly overstepped his authority and officiously overruled or stealthily undermined them. In fact, throughout Brigham's time as territorial governor, federal officials complained to the administration in Washington that he was a megalomaniac who thwarted their authority every chance he got.

Brigham countered that the federal officials were hopelessly corrupt and focused mainly on accumulating personal fortunes through the abuse of their official power. He maintained that graft, bribes, thievery, and embezzlement ran rampant among them. In truth, corruption among federally appointed officials in the West did run high; misappropriation of funds was common; Native Americans, especially, were often shorted on supplies and materials meant to benefit them. Skimming of U.S. Army funds and supplies was also a common practice of avaricious federal appointees and agents.

Two things brought the conflict between Brigham and the federal officials to a head shortly after Buchanan's inauguration in March of 1857. First came a formal protest sent to Buchanan by the Utah Territory legislature, which was controlled by the Mormons, and therefore by Brigham. The territorial legislature aired their grievances against the federal appointees, especially the judges charged with adjudicating policy fairly and meting out justice equitably for all residents of the Utah Territory. The Mormon legislators claimed that the federal officials did not act impartially, but oppressed Mormons, inflicting biased judgments upon them. The legislature went so far as to state that the Mormons of Utah would send away any more corrupt federal officials sent to rule them by Washington, D.C. Brigham had instigated and given his full support to this unwise act of the legislature—a belligerent statement full of complaints and near-threats.

Buchanan's foolish overreaction to the Utah legislature's folly precipitated the Utah War. The strong language the legislature had used inspired a barrage of letters to him from disaffected former federal officials in the Utah Territory, alleging that Brigham Young, the Mormon legislators, and the Mormon population in general had interfered with their duties and undermined their authority. These letters, couched in strong terms, detailed the kinds of abuses that had arisen in the Utah Territory. One letter from an ex-judge named W. W. Drummond asserted that everyone in Utah held their life at the whim of Brigham Young and that the Mormons murdered, robbed, castrated, and imprisoned non-Mormons who disagreed with them. But Drummond had his own issues: he had arrived in Utah with a prostitute on his arm, having left his wife and children back home in Illinois. To Brigham and his Mormon followers, this caddish behavior compromised the man.

Still, there was some truth to Drummond's letter. In the mid-1850s, Brigham had instituted a reform movement in the church that had resulted in increased religious fervor. That fervor spilled over from enthusiastic repentance and righteousness to vigorous acting out against sinners and infidels. The religious emotionalism led to violence against some church members and also against non-Mormons, among whom the reform movement naturally raised anxiety. At this time, Brigham openly advanced his doctrine of "blood atonement." Brigham taught that while animal sacrifice in the temple had paid for sins committed in ancient times, this animal sacrifice had given way to the ultimate sacrifice paid by Jesus Christ on the cross for humankind's sins. But according to Brigham, the crucifixion no longer atoned for all sins, and sinners now had to pay for their transgressions with their own blood. This doctrine justified the righteous in maiming sinners and even taking their lives for the sinners' own good—to preserve their chance of heavenly salvation through all eternity.

Brigham's wayward "blood atonement" theology created a deadly violent climate in Utah. Instances of murder occurred, including by hanging. And at least one poor man—Thomas Lewis of Manti, an excommunicated Saint in his early twenties who had emigrated from Britain—underwent castration on the order of a church elder, his bishop Warren Snow. The bishop may have had personal motives, arising from his and Lewis's mutual interest in the same woman, for issuing the castration order. Then again, Lewis himself did have a pronounced tendency to violence; he had recently assaulted a member of the community, a man named John Price, with a shovel and nearly killed him. Next Lewis had clashed with his brother-in-law Isaac Vorhees and threatened to kill him. Vorhees had recourse to the law, and Lewis was sentenced to a five-year prison term. But on the way to prison on October 29, 1856, Lewis was waylaid and kidnapped by a group of vigilantes who hauled him from the wagon that was transporting him, threw him to the ground, covered his head with a blanket, and removed his testicles.

Lewis's incensed mother, Elizabeth Jones, whom Brigham would years later take as a plural wife, wrote to Brigham in protest. According to her letter, her son, after being clipped like a pig, was abandoned in the desert where he nearly died of exposure and loss of blood before being found two days later. Brigham replied to Lewis's mother in the spirit of the doctrine of blood atonement: he wrote that he would rather have his child's life terminated than have the child's chance at heavenly salvation for all eternity forfeited. And half a year later, when church elders called into question Warren Snow's judgment and discretion in issuing the castration order, Brigham defended Snow, and Snow retained his rank as a bishop.

Brigham's theology grew increasingly repugnant, despotic, and vindictive: he argued that dead sinners whose lives were terminated by the righteous would be unable to commit more sins and thereby ruin their chance at eternal bliss in heaven. Such "theology" is manifestly not in concert with the teachings of Christ on mercy and forgiveness. Brigham's heated preaching of the concept of blood atonement frightened many Mormons. His theology was getting further and further removed from traditional Christianity. Brigham would go on to posit the theory that Adam was God. The church would eventually have to discard Brigham's more bizarre beliefs, just as it would have to discard the doctrines of polygamy and blood atonement.

The conflict between Mormons and federal officials in the Utah Territory was the first crisis in the Buchanan presidency, and it struck before he could even acclimate himself to his big new job as chief executive. And the problem in Utah had larger implications. The issue of slave versus free states, which involved questions of states' rights and popular sovereignty, had extended now to territories. There had recently been fierce clashes in "bleeding Kansas" over whether that state should be slave or free. The Democrats espoused local governance in their popular sovereignty policy to appease the slave-holding states in the South. The Republicans repudiated the Democratic policy of popular sovereignty, considering it a pernicious dodge that only enabled the peculiar institution of slavery to continue. Who would have the final say? The states and the territories? Or the federal government? The conflict between the Utah Mormons and the federal government under Buchanan in the spring of 1857 heated up right as the scalding national debate over states' rights versus centralized federal jurisdiction was raging nearly out of control. Indeed, in only four short years, the Civil War would break out over this very issue.

Listening to foolish advisors, Buchanan leaped to the conclusion that the Mormons in Utah had adopted an overly aggressive interpretation of popular sovereignty, proved themselves disloyal to the federal government, and proclaimed themselves independent of the United States. This foolish cadre of advisors to Buchanan saw in the conflict with Utah, a mere territory, a chance to escalate and then easily win a crisis that would divert attention away from the incendiary nationwide showdown brewing over the issue of slavery and states' rights.

In consequence, Buchanan blundered. In March of 1857, he foolishly issued an order for an army of twenty-five hundred troops to march into the Utah Territory to reassert federal control. Significantly, Texas senator Sam Houston, like Brigham Young a titan of western exploration and colonization, strenuously opposed Buchanan's impulsive order. Houston considered sending an army a serious overreaction to a manageable dispute and said so publicly, but to no avail.

Ignoring Senator Houston, Buchanan took this potentially catastrophic action without so much as exchanging a letter or word with territorial governor Brigham Young. Attempts made by John Berhisel, Brigham's emissary in Washington, to smooth the situation and defuse the crisis failed absolutely. Buchanan had made up his mind, and he wasn't going to change it. Brigham only learned of Buchanan's order to dispatch a federal army to the Utah Territory from newspaper accounts and from letters sent by friends and representatives living back east.

Given the murderous misuse of state militias against the Mormons in Missouri and in Illinois, it is little wonder that Brigham and the Saints overreacted once they learned that Buchanan had dispatched an "army" to invade and occupy the Utah Territory and subdue the Mormons. The Saints assumed that once again they were in for a round of violence, murder, rape, and other assorted forms of abuse. The collective Mormon memory was full of vivid pictures of past persecution. (Their mood was further inflamed by the recent murder of elder Parley Pratt in Arkansas, where he had been doing missionary work when he was shot and stabbed by the jilted husband of a plural wife he had taken.) Brigham Young—angry, defiant, and, somewhat justifiably paranoid—ordered the Nauvoo Legion to full strength and all Mormons to prepare themselves to withstand a siege and battle back.

Brigham arranged for ammunition to be shipped from St. Louis to the various Mormon settlements in the Utah Territory. He also put out a general alert to clean and repair firearms, to sharpen scythes for use as bayonets, and to strop old swords to ready them for action. He also ordered heavy recruitment to the Nauvoo Legion. Some males as young as fourteen joined the local militias and started training, as did some others as old as sixty. Daniel Wells, appointed by Brigham to head up the Nauvoo Legion, toured the outlying Mormon settlements and trained local militias.

As things turned out, the "war" principally took the form of Mormon skirmishes against the federal army as it traveled west from its assembly point at Fort Leavenworth in Kansas under Colonel Albert S. Johnston. (This is the same Albert S. Johnston who, as a Confederate general five years later at the famous Civil War Battle of Shiloh in 1862, would be shot in the thigh astride his horse and bleed out quickly from a severed artery.) Johnston and his expeditionary force, not really large enough to constitute a proper army, would be frustrated by brilliant Mormon harassing tactics that amounted to guerrilla warfare.

The Mormons disrupted the federal army's supply lines and scorched the grazing lands needed by their horses and other livestock as they headed west. Mormon raiders also stole or sabotaged the federal army's provisions. Ironically, the Mormons were applying the very form of guerrilla warfare the American colonists had used so successfully against the British. And the Americans in the Revolutionary War in turn had the Native Americans to thank for this kind of expertise in guerilla warfare by a lesser but more mobile force against a greater but less mobile army.

In Brigham's all-out effort to protect his people and their new religious kingdom, he actually recruited Native Americans to join the

Mormon militias in repelling the invading federals. He vowed to burn
Salt Lake City to the ground if necessary to prevent the federal army from
taking charge of the Mormon community, church, and kingdom. But
Brigham had no desire to become another Mormon martyr like his men-
tor Joseph Smith. Brigham announced that in the event the federal army
threatened his capture—which could result in his hanging, if the rumor
he had heard proved true—he would flee into the wilderness, thwarting
his enemies, and continue to work for the church and the kingdom.

Many regrettable events occurred on both sides during the sixteen
months of the so-called Utah War. Buchanan and the entire federal
government did not come off well. But Brigham was directly or indirectly responsible for actions that hurt the Mormon cause. Brigham, for
example, declared martial law, and in combination with the lingering
fervor from the mid-1850s reformation, the hysteria incited by martial
law fomented an atmosphere of fear, paranoia, panic, and righteous
anger among the Mormons. War fever is notorious for prompting
atrocities; a threat to their very existence tends to undermine people's
better judgment.

Brigham's war rhetoric, especially in a situation of martial law after
he had put the militias on ready alert, prompted fearful and misguided
Mormons to carry out atrocities against real and imagined enemies
during the months when they feared invasion by the federal army. Yet
the federal army was delayed so many times in its approach from the
east that it never clashed head-on with the Mormon militias. In the end,
a brokered peace agreement aborted the potential battle Brigham had
expected to wage with the invaders in Echo Canyon, which Brigham had
directed the Nauvoo Legion to fortify so that it would be a death trap
for the invading federal troops. Brigham had gone so far as to recruit an
auxiliary mounted force of two thousand Mormon riflemen to reinforce
the Nauvoo Legion in defending Echo Canyon; it would have been a

turkey shoot if the federal army tried to enter it to gain access to the Great Salt Lake Valley.

But the federal army was late in leaving Fort Leavenworth and had to travel twelve hundred miles to reach Echo Canyon, so the showdown never happened. Like the ill-fated Donner Party, the army started its long western trek too late and was stymied by the onset of winter. By the time the army arrived on the eastern edge of the Utah Territory, Brigham had organized his defense and Colonel Johnston had no choice but to stop just inside the eastern boundary at Ham's Fork and camp for the winter. Even though the big showdown in Echo Canyon never materialized, while the federals were en route and then encamped in their winter quarters awaiting the spring thaw, events unfolded in the Utah Territory that redounded ultimately to the injury of the Saints.

The worst of these events was the tragic Mountain Meadows Massacre.

CHAPTER 24

THE MOUNTAIN MEADOWS · MASSACRE

The Mountain Meadows Massacre is the ugliest stain on the collective soul of the Mormons in their entire history. As part of his imposition of martial law, Brigham had unwisely declared that no one could pass through the Utah Territory without obtaining prior written permission. The Mormons still harbored resentment against the wagon trains originating in Missouri because of the horrible treatment accorded Mormons in Missouri twenty years earlier, and also because many wagon trains of Missourians that the Mormons had encountered on the Oregon Trail had perpetuated this shabby and abusive treatment of Mormons.

As governor, Brigham was also the head of Indian Affairs. For years he had mostly acted diplomatically to ensure peaceful coexistence between the Native Americans and the Mormons as, for example, in resolving the Walker War in the summer of 1853 by sitting down with

Chief Walker and other tribal elders, working out differences, and smok-
ing a peace pipe. Yet ever since the Mormons had arrived in the Great
Salt Lake Valley in 1847, there had been clashes that sometimes got out
of hand and often involved fatalities—when, for instance, the Mormons
and the Indians contended too heatedly over hunting, fishing, grazing,
and water rights. As we have seen, there were exceptions to Brigham's
generally admirable diplomacy toward Indians, most notably his barbaric lapse in judgment in sanctioning the slaughter of eleven unarmed
Ute warriors near Provo in January of 1850.

But now, with the onset of a possible invasion by the federal army,
Brigham encouraged the Native Americans to attack wagon trains of
outsiders, the non-Mormon pioneers passing through the Utah Territory. At the same time, the smaller militia forces of the outlying Mormon
communities also became more aggressive against outsiders, including
these wagon trains of non-Mormon pioneers passing through. Fomenting war fever is always dangerous. The result is nearly always murderous
chaos. This time was no different.

From late July to early September of 1857, Brigham's anger
increased, and the rhetoric in his war sermons amounted to a call to
arms. Frustrated with federal interference and irked by even the small
permanent U.S. Army presence in the territory, Brigham spoke out
about the need for Mormon independence and self-rule. He claimed
that God had directed the Saints to establish their kingdom in Utah and
that was what they were going to do in the face of an invasion by a
federal army destined to augment the small army presence already
stationed within the territory. More federal troops in Utah meant less
Mormon self-rule.

By late summer that year, the southern Utah Nauvoo Legion was
on ready alert and fully prepared to carry out Brigham's directives. He
had forbidden Mormons to aid the non-Mormons passing through the
territory, but also according to Brigham's instructions, the Mormon

militias were not to attack these non-Mormon emigrants either. On the other hand, Brigham had specified that whatever the Indians did to wayfaring wagon trains of non-Mormon pioneers was not to be interfered with by Mormon militias. Brigham was acting disingenuously. He had incited the Indians against the non-Mormons by telling them that the non-Mormons intended to invade the territory with an army that would attack and kill Mormons and then turn around and do the same thing to the Indians. The Indians, who had always made a distinction between the Mormons and non-Mormon Americans, sided with Brigham and the Mormons, who had generally treated them better than had the U.S. Army, the chief interface between the Indians and the non-Mormon Americans. A southern Utah tribe called the Paiutes had an especially strong alliance with the Mormons.

The Mountain Meadows Massacre occurred over the course of five days, from Monday, September 7, through Friday, September 11, 1857. Mountain Meadows is a valley at the southern end of the Wasatch Range and at the beginning of the last stretch of the Old Spanish Trail, the southern wagon train route to California. A wagon train of pioneers mostly from Arkansas had pulled into Salt Lake City in late July and not met with the usual Mormon hospitality. Brigham had sternly directed Mormon merchants not to sell supplies to wagon trains of non-Mormons passing through.

This ill-fated wagon train came to be known as the Baker-Fancher Party, after two of its leaders. The wagon train had about 125 members, give or take fifteen. It was well-organized, well-led, and quite prosperous, including a couple hundred head of cattle being transported to its southern California destination. By early September, the Baker-Fancher Party had pushed on, covered 250 miles since leaving Salt Lake City, and reached Mountain Meadows, a beautiful grazing and camping area near Cedar City in Iron County, in the southwestern corner of Utah, some forty miles from the Nevada border. The Baker-Fancher Party hoped to rest up at Mountain Meadows and resupply in Cedar City for the final push to San Bernardino.

But in southern Utah, religious fervor and war fever were cresting. From the beginning, there were problems between the Baker-Fancher Party and the overwrought local Mormons. Colonel William H. Dame of Parowan, a local militia commander, following Brigham Young's directive, refused to sell supplies to the non-Mormon wagon train. When one local Mormon named William Leany fed a member of the Baker-Fancher party, Dame ordered him beaten. Animosity between the local Mormons and the wayfaring non-Mormons ran high, and arguments broke out. In nearby Cedar City, the Arkansas pioneers grew angry and hostile when they were again refused supplies by Mormon merchants. The members of the wagon train were hungry and desperately needed provisions. They may have threatened Cedar City's mayor, Isaac Haight, and its bishop, Philip Klingensmith, a blacksmith by trade.

The local militia leaders held a series of meetings to determine how to deal with the increasingly obstreperous members of the Baker-Fancher Party. Cedar City mayor Isaac Haight was also the district stake president and a major in the Nauvoo Legion. He dispatched a rider, militiaman James Haslam, on Sunday evening, September 6, with a letter for Young in Salt Lake City, seeking advice. Round trip on horseback totaled five hundred miles and took a week. An exhausted Haslam reached Salt Lake City on Thursday, September 10, and arrived back in Cedar City bearing Brigham's letter of advice on Sunday, September 13. Young's letter reiterated his policy of instructing the Mormons to let the non-Mormons pass through in peace but to stand back and do nothing if the Indians decided to attack. In any case, by the time Haslam arrived back in Cedar City, the massacre had already happened.

During the week when Haslam was in transit, Haight took matters into his own hands. He ordered John D. Lee, a friend of Brigham Young and a member of the Iron County militia, to recruit the Paiute Indians

THE MOUNTAIN MEADOWS MASSACRE 197

to launch a raid on the Baker-Fancher wagon train, which was an especially attractive target because it included the large herd of cattle and
was also well-supplied with tools, clothing, and household goods. When
the Paiute Indians attacked the encamped wagon train on Monday,
September 7, Lee and several other local Mormon militiamen joined in,
all disguised as Indians.

A shootout and standoff were the initial results of the attack. The
Arkansans drew their wagons into a tight circle, chained them together,
and heaped dirt beneath the wagons and into their cargo beds to sink
them into the ground and form a makeshift earthwork, from behind
which the pioneers returned the invaders' fire. In the intervals of a series
of pitched battles that followed, the stouthearted pioneers buried their
dead within the circle formed by the wagons. Over the course of a four-
day siege, the Paiutes, though they had rustled most of the cattle, started
to lose heart at the difficulty of subduing the brave Arkansans.

Local Mormon militia leaders Colonel Dame and Major Haight were
also becoming frustrated—and fearful of the consequences should the
Mormon instigation of and participation in the attack become known.
They became afraid that the besieged pioneers had recognized white
men attacking them alongside the Indians. There was also the possibility that another wagon train would come along and witness the Mormon
treachery.

To eliminate any possibility that the Mormons' involvement would
be discovered, Dame and Haight ordered Lee to work the same double-
cross that the Mormons had employed in January of 1850 near Provo,
slaughtering the eleven Ute warriors who surrendered and disarmed
only to be mowed down in a hail of bullets the following morning. On
Friday, September 11, Lee and two other militiamen, waving a white flag,
approached the entrenched pioneers, who were just about out of ammunition and food. Lee tricked them into surrendering under false assurances, telling them that otherwise he feared further and more ferocious

attacks would be mounted against them by the savage Indians, who no doubt would bring in reinforcements. Lee told the pioneers they could escape and continue their journey in safety if they cooperated.

Lee and his militiamen then marched all the unarmed male pioneers a mile away from the dug-in wagons. John Higbee, another major in the Cedar City militia and a leader in planning the whole operation, then shouted for everyone to halt. At a quick signal from Higbee, the militiamen raked the pioneers with gunfire, killing every unarmed male in cold blood, lest accounts of this attack leak out and incite violence and trouble for the Mormons. Back at the campsite, the Paiutes meanwhile scalped and killed all the women and also killed all the children above the age of reason so that they could not testify as witnesses to this atrocity. Seventeen infants and toddlers were spared and placed in the homes of local Mormons. Years later, these surviving children would be retrieved by the U.S. Army and returned to the homes of their Arkansas relatives.

The mass murder at Mountain Meadows is among the worst in American history. It is understandable in the light of Mormon paranoia as a result of previous persecution, but it is certainly not blameless. Paranoia mixed with war fever is inevitably a volatile prescription for senseless violence and wholesale murder, and in this case the toxic mixture created an American atrocity.

CHAPTER 25

THE AFTERMATH

— OF THE —

ATROCITY

Historians have argued for over a century and a half about whether Brigham Young knew and approved the Mountain Meadows Massacre in advance. Probably he did not, though a slight chance exists that he did. He did, however, without a doubt create the atmosphere that inflamed the Mormon paranoia and hostility to outsiders that made it likely. At this juncture in his life, Brigham had lost the equilibrium, restraint, and diplomacy that had characterized his leadership up to his appointment as territorial governor in 1850. The threat of yet another incursion from a hostile military force evoked in Brigham and in many other older Mormons memories of atrocities and massacres perpetrated against them by the state militias in Missouri and in Illinois, most notably the Haun's Mill Massacre in 1838, where at least seventeen Mormons were murdered by Missouri militiamen.

These murderous state militias had not been restrained by federal forces, a form of succor the Mormons had pleaded for in vain with government officials in Washington, D.C. Now the Mormons were faced with invasion by a hostile federal force, and the strain had broken them. Incited by war rhetoric, the strained and panicky Mormons resorted to senseless violence. There are still people in Arkansas to this day who detest Mormons for planning and carrying out this slaughter against innocent people from their state, in some instances their relatives. Besides the damage to the Mormons' reputation in Arkansas, many non-Mormon Americans regarded this mass murder as proof that Mormons were a dangerous sect, not to be trusted. That bad feeling lingers in many quarters even down to today, especially west of the Mississippi.

After the massacre, the Utah Mormons immediately launched a clumsy and ineffective cover-up. Brigham led this campaign, realizing that widespread knowledge of this atrocity could trigger massive retaliatory violence against the Mormons and their church. The first Mormon line of defense, an obvious dodge, was to fix all the blame for the massacre on the Paiutes. Brigham dispatched a letter to the commissioner of Indian Affairs asserting that Native Americans had carried out the slaughter. At the time, he knew this was a bold-faced lie.

But the truth eventually came out. For one thing, John D. Lee immediately started to talk, prompted most likely by a guilty conscience. The continuation of the "Utah War" into the next year set back a federal investigation of the massacre until the following year of 1859, when both U.S. Army Brevet Major James Henry Carleton and Commissioner of Indian Affairs Jacob Forney, after conducting separate investigations and on-site inspections and interviews, concluded that the Paiute Indians had been aided in this atrocity by Mormon militiamen. Carleton made a damning assessment of the severity of the slaughter, characterizing the massacre as a "heinous crime" and reporting that the sight of the bones of children found still clutching their mothers' skeleton was something he could never forget.

In March of that same year, a newly appointed federal judge, John Candlebaugh, convened a grand jury in Provo. Candlebaugh tried to arrest John D. Lee, Isaac Haight, and John Higbee, but all three hid out and evaded arrest. But that didn't stop the plain-spoken Judge Candlebaugh from condemning these three miscreants—and attributing blame to Brigham Young as an accessory before the fact for creating such an overwrought and unstable climate. To protect Brigham, a Mormon probate court judge named Elias Smith arrested him under a territorial warrant, hoping he could stand trial in a friendly territorial court under Mormon jurisdiction rather than in a federal court. When the federal authorities did not issue charges against Brigham, the judge released him.

The Civil War intervened, and no proper federal investigation could be mounted until the mid-seventies. In 1875, John D. Lee's first trial ended in a hung jury, but he was detained and tried again. The following year, a mostly Mormon jury convicted Lee at his second trial. The clinching factor in his conviction was the testimony of Philip Kingensmith, the former Cedar City bishop and blacksmith who had received immunity in a plea bargain. By the time of the Lee trial, Klingensmith had renounced his Mormon faith, left the church, and moved to Nevada. While on trial, Lee also gave testimony incriminating several of his fellow murderers, all of whom were hiding out from federal authorities.

In John D. Lee's later remarks after his conviction, he claimed he was a "scapegoat" for higher church authorities. He was sentenced to death and given a choice, in accordance with Utah law, of being hanged, beheaded, or executed by firing squad. He was duly executed for his role in the massacre by firing squad in March of 1877 while seated next to his open coffin in a field in Mountain Meadows. Many other of Lee's fellow Mormon mass murderers, the ones who had fled and hidden out, thwarted justice. This did not sit well with many non-Mormons or with the national press, who had never forgotten the massacre despite the interruption of the Civil War and through the long years until the Lee trials in the mid-seventies. Brigham Young was never tried in a court of law, but despite a Mormon public relations campaign to exonerate him, the mass murder at Mountain Meadows remains the darkest stain on his reputation and on that of Mormons in general.

The Mountain Meadows Massacre was by far the most horrendous tragedy in the destabilized conditions during the "Utah War," but other regrettable incidents involving loss of life also occurred. After they entered northern Utah Territory, a group of six men traveling east from California known to history as the Aiken Party were arrested by Nauvoo Legion militiamen on suspicion of being spies for the invading federal army encamped hundreds of miles distant on the eastern edge of the territory. The theory that these Californians were spies was groundless and bizarre even at the time. Only murky evidence exists for exactly what happened next, but the upshot was that members of the Nauvoo Legion murdered five of the six men. The lone survivor escaped back to California.

In another outbreak of violence in the Utah Territory during this conflict, a tribe of Native Americans called the Bannocks attacked a Mormon settlement at Fort Lemhi in what is now southern Idaho but was then the Oregon Territory. The Bannocks murdered two Mormon missionaries, wounded five others, and rustled hundreds of head of cattle.

Fortunately for everyone in Utah, cooler heads eventually prevailed. After Brigham and other church elders had vacated Salt Lake City in the face of the invading army and taken refuge forty miles south in Provo, and while Albert S. Johnston, promoted now to general, waited out winter 1858 with his army in Ham's Fork, Philadelphia lawyer Thomas L. Kane, a great friend to the Mormons, interceded. Kane used his considerable political influence in Washington to persuade

Buchanan to empower him to travel west and broker a peace with Brigham Young and his Mormon followers. Assuming greater responsibility and authority than the president had in fact given him, Kane used his imagination and daring to defuse a potentially disfiguring calamity for a young nation still in its first century, a calamity that could have besmirched everything that young nation stood for.

Dedicated to disarmament and peace, Kane worked toward a compromise and reason prevailed. He convinced Brigham Young to allow the army to enter the Great Salt Lake Valley in spring to set up a permanent federal installation; to allow Alfred Cumming, a non-Mormon Georgian overly fond of strong drink, to replace Brigham as governor of the Utah Territory; and to permit other properly appointed federal officials to carry out their judicial and administrative duties unimpeded. In exchange, Brigham received assurances that his followers would not be harmed, that his church members could worship as they deemed proper, and that a general pardon would be granted to Brigham and to all Mormons who had resisted the federal authorities in any way that could be regarded as disloyal, seditious, or treasonous.

Neither Brigham nor Buchanan won the "war." They both lost: in Brigham's case, power; and in Buchanan's case, dignity. As a result of the war, Brigham would never again reign in the Utah Territory in the secular sphere with the same reach and authority as in the ecclesiastical realm. As part of the peace agreement that averted a potentially tragic and very real war, Brigham and the Mormons had to agree to let non-resident federal appointees administer civil and judicial authority in the territory. What's more, the Mormons had to accept that, as a condition of amnesty and pardon, the U.S. Army could build Fort Floyd, forty miles from Salt Lake City.

At the time Fort Floyd was constructed and named for then Secretary of War John B. Floyd, it was the largest military garrison in the nation. Later, after the peace agreement had aborted an actual war, and following the removal of Brigham Young as governor, Secretary Floyd boasted that once sufficient federal force had been brought to bear, the Mormons had set aside their bluster and bravado and been quickly reduced to a state of submission.

That was not entirely true, but Brigham's defiance had proved rash and futile, as chest-beating and saber-rattling usually do. The net result was that Brigham lost his political power and declined from the nearly omnipotent leader he had been. He should never have defied the federal government and called out the Mormon militias to interdict the U.S. Army on its way into the Great Salt Lake Valley. Power had gone to his head, and the depredations suffered by Mormons had fueled his anger and built his frustration to the point where he lost perspective.

Yet for the remaining nineteen years of his life, even though Brigham had lost his power in the civil government of Utah, he would be totally revered by his Mormon followers. Though stripped of his power in secular matters, he remained a kind of ecclesiastical potentate in his desert kingdom.

He also became internationally famous, though mostly for the wrong reason: he was something of a curiosity on account of the vast number of his wives and children. His avid practice of polygamy drew massive publicity to him and to his church for nearly three and a half decades after Brigham was ousted as governor, until 1890, fifteen years after Brigham's death, when the church renounced the practice. Most of this publicity was negative, and it prevented Utah from attaining statehood until 1896, thirty-nine years after Buchanan's—and Brigham's—blunder.

CHAPTER 26

POLYGAMY

For nearly half a century, the doctrine and practice of polygamy caused problems, both internally and externally, for Mormons. The vast majority of Americans in mostly monogamous Protestant America in the nineteenth century deemed the practice of polygamy unacceptable and offensive. Many of Joseph Smith's own followers had recoiled from this practice when Smith declared it a new doctrine of the church in the early 1840s. Polygamy would lead to defections and schisms within the church for years to come and, as word of the practice leaked out into the general population, it only intensified the already negative opinion most non-Mormons held of the Mormons.

There is an old injunction against speaking of sex, politics, and religion in polite society. But when it comes to Mormonism and the practice of polygamy, it is utterly impossible to avoid discussing any of these three verboten subjects. Whether Joseph Smith was spiritually impelled to declare polygamy a religious doctrine or if he embraced plural marriage for baser motives is a matter of opinion. But if Mormon polygamy may have been about sex, religion certainly came into as well. The Mormons did not just practice polygamy; they held it as a theological doctrine. And it was politics that both put a stop to the practice and eventually changed the theology.

Polygamy was outlawed in the United States first during the Lincoln administration in 1862 under the Morrill Anti-Bigamy Act. Then, twenty years later, under President Chester A. Arthur, the Edmunds Act reinforced the Morrill Act. Under the Edmunds Act, polygamists forfeited the right to vote, were declared ineligible for jury duty, and were barred from holding public office; many of them, including many high-ranking Mormons, were jailed.

Recent court cases have revisited the practice of polygamy in the United States—some of them involving Mormons or splinter groups that have split off from the Mormons, often characterized as "fundamentalist Mormons." But the history of polygamy as an institution of mainstream Mormonism covers a half century of controversy and problems from 1840 until 1890, when the Mormon Church officially renounced the doctrine of polygamy.

The first instance of Joseph Smith's publicly engaging in an extramarital relationship occurred in the mid-1830s when he had a dalliance with a servant girl named Fanny Alger. There have been claims that he raped her. No "endowment" ceremony, no "sealing," and no "celestial marriage" took place with her, and she left the relationship by 1836 and married a non-Mormon. Smith's legal wife Emma was upset by her husband's infidelity and let him know it. So, too, did high-ranking elders of the new religion that Smith had founded, most notably Oliver Cowdery, who was one of the original "Three Witnesses" to the golden tablets Smith received from the angel Moroni and translated into *The Book of Mormon*.

Cowdery accused Smith of adultery; he saw the whole affair with Fanny Alger as sordid and unseemly.

By the spring of 1841, Joseph Smith took his first "plural wife" when he was "sealed" to the daughter of an old family friend. So as not to draw attention to the sealing ceremony, the bride, Louisa Beaman, wore a man's overcoat and hat as a disguise. Smith insisted that plural marriages had to be "sealed" under church auspices for the couple to be eligible to live happily ever after in eternity, in heaven, in a "celestial marriage." Over the years Smith elaborated various theological doctrines to explain and justify plural marriage. The basic theology justifying polygamy was that the church had to "endow" and "seal" the polygamous couple to ensure that the man and woman so joined could live on forever in heaven as part of the man's celestial family. The woman could be sealed to the man "in time" or "in time and in eternity."

The "in time"-only plural wives may not have been engaged in conjugal activities with the husband. Apparently, when a man was sealed "in time" only, and not "in eternity," he would undertake to provide for a widow and her children solely as a protector and benefactor, in a practice of Christian kindness and mercy without any sexual relations between the man and the sealed widow. This was an admirable Mormon practice toward women abandoned in the harsh frontier West in the nineteenth century, when such women had scant or no means to support themselves or their fatherless children.

It seems that the "in eternity" brides did engage in conjugal activity with their husbands. There was also another variation of plural marriage where a husband would be a "proxy," as when Brigham Young was sealed to plural wives of Joseph Smith after Smith's death and Brigham enjoyed conjugal relations with these women though they were destined to spend eternity as plural wives of Joseph Smith as part of Smith's celestial family, not as part of Brigham's celestial family.

Later in the spring of 1841, after Joseph Smith was sealed to Louisa Beaman, his first plural wife, he disclosed the doctrine of plural marriage to his Apostles, newly returned from the mission to England, including Brigham Young, who, like most of the other Apostles, recoiled from it. But after several months of Smith's persuasion, Brigham accepted the doctrine, as did most of the other Apostles, though not all. Plural marriage would divide the church from within throughout the years it was practiced. Upon Smith's announcement of plural marriage, some Apostles left and formed their own new religions, usually based on Mormonism as it had existed before Smith introduced plural marriage.

The Mormons also call plural marriage by other names, such as "eternal marriage," "celestial marriage," "patriarchal marriage," "spiritual wifery," and a few others. Over the years, the doctrine of plural marriage evolved more features, rituals, and theological justifications as Smith and then Brigham Young, after Smith's death, added them. Essentially the "endowment" ceremony "sealed" the covenant between the man and his plural wife and could lead, under ideal conditions, to the couple living in eternity in celestial bliss as a "king" and a "queen."

Early on, there was trouble when Smith attempted to persuade a comely seventeen-year-old emigrant from England named Martha Brotherton to become his plural wife. Brigham joined Smith in the effort to acquire her assent. She declined the honor and wrote about it, causing anti-Mormon sentiment to rise. Other women over the years spoke out against polygamy as well. As we have seen, Sidney Rigdon, Smith's close associate and advisor, never accepted plural marriage and decamped to Pittsburgh and started his own religion without it. And William Law, another elder and close associate of Smith, protested polygamy, worked against it, and left the church to form his own religion in Texas, again without the doctrine and practice of polygamy.

As word leaked out about this practice after Smith formalized it as doctrine in Nauvoo in the early 1840s, hostility toward Mormons in

Illinois escalated. After the assassination of Smith in 1844, Brigham Young stepped up the practice of polygamy both personally and within the church. Before the exodus to the West, in the final months in Nauvoo, once the temple was complete, Brigham set about endowing and sealing single and plural marriages at a rapid pace. He also took many plural wives himself at that time, and increased this activity a year later while encamped at Winter Quarters on the great exodus west.

As defectors and dissenters spoke out against the new doctrine of polygamy, disaffection toward the Mormons grew among non-Mormons. Monogamous nineteenth-century Americans simply would not accept the practice. They considered it tribal, primitive, and against the traditional theology of the Judeo-Christian Bible and its legacy. Non-Mormons critics of the practice rejected it despite Smith citing theological arguments that polygamy was grounded in the Biblical practices of the Hebrew patriarchs. Smith always argued that he was harking back in his new religion to the true core of the earliest Biblical practices and traditions.

Americans almost unanimously rejected Smith's arguments. Besides the protests of women defectors from Mormon plural marriages, a man named John Cook Bennett gained access to the Mormons, perhaps by briefly joining or feigning to join the church, and then published what was considered an expose of Mormon polygamy. Sex, as always—even in nineteenth-century Protestant America—sold newspapers, magazines, and books, especially whenever it was presented salaciously. Bennett came through on both counts and toured widely and successfully, promoting his best-selling book. Non-Mormons' negative reaction to polygamy added to the "otherness" and the "cult" aspects of the Mormons, augmenting the always dangerous divide between "us" and "them." It incited the same sort of violence and persecution as burst forth from the nativist Americans a few years later when the xenophobic Know-Nothings attacked the Catholics, another religious minority feared as bloc voters dangerously under the sway of priestcraft—and in their case foreign, Roman influence.

From the late 1840s onward, settled in Utah as leader of the church, Brigham Young practiced polygamy avidly. So, too, did many other Mormon elders, especially after Brigham made the doctrine a matter of public record in 1852. The Mormons then added polygamy to the roster of arguments for popular sovereignty, or states' rights, to trump centralized government under federal control in Washington. In arguing for popular sovereignty the Mormons aligned themselves with the slave-owning states in the South. It's worth noting that just as most Southerners did not own slaves, most Mormons did not practice polygamy. In both instances it was society's upper crust, the wealthy landowners or the well-heeled elders and community leaders, who indulged in these peculiar practices.

The practice of polygamy—especially polygyny, where there is one husband and many wives—has been shown to impose gender inequities on the women involved, usually in the form of psychological and emotional deprivation. This sad fact holds true for the children in such domestic arrangements, too. In huge polygamous families, the children suffer psychological and emotional hardships, just as their mothers do. Documentation exists to verify that much of this kind of deprivation occurred in Brigham Young's family. As is usual in polygamous arrangements, older wives were often slighted in favor of younger wives. Spats, resentments, and rivalries were also common among the plural wives. When Brigham built the Beehive House and the Lion House in Salt Lake City in the early 1850s, he was more or less warehousing his wives and children, some of whom refused these communal accommodations and insisted on separate quarters. In the last fifteen years or so of his life, Brigham tried to right this wrong by providing each wife with an individual domicile for herself and her children.

Significantly, there is no record or even hint of Brigham ever having laid a hand on his wives or his children in anger. By all accounts, he was a loving husband and provider and, given his inherent limitations as one man with dozens of children, a caring father. His letters to his sons are tender and solicitous and full of good and caring advice. His generosity to his wives is a matter of historical record. But jealousy among the wives was impossible to avoid. There was resentment of Mary Ann Angell's exalted status, and Brigham clearly had a special place in his heart for Mary Ann and for his children by her. Brigham was deeply affected when he lost his young daughter Mary Ann when she was still a small child, and when her sister Luna died an untimely death as a young woman, he wrote about fighting off a depression threatening to overwhelm him. Bear in mind: Brigham had lost his adored mother at a tender age and his beloved first wife Miriam Works after only a few short years of happy married life; moreover, he doted on his two eldest daughters by Miriam, Elizabeth and Vilate.

Still, he couldn't make everyone happy all the time. The wives in Salt Lake City vied for favors and for preferment. They wanted more for themselves and for their children. If any other wife received more atten-tion, more money, or better accommodations for her and her family, resentments arose. There were serial jealousies as Brigham embraced ever younger and ever more beautiful wives when he was in his fifties and sixties. Amelia Folsom, one of his last wives, a remarkable beauty, fairly wrapped the grandfatherly but still vital Brigham around her little finger, as comely young women are wont to do. Brigham's susceptibility prompted sarcasm and contempt from the older and now displaced wives who felt they'd been put out to pasture.

Was he understanding even then, with so much criticism raining down on him from so many disgruntled former brides? Apparently so: he granted divorces to several wives, and he endeavored to solve any problems he could for any others who came to him distraught and seeking his help. For years he put up with a steady stream of poison pen letters from Augusta Adams Cobb, a Boston Brahmin beauty he had married but whose romantic expectations he could not meet, especially once he'd taken up with nubile beauties young enough to be Augusta's daughters. There is something to be said for the managerial skills and charm of a man capable of sitting down to supper with sixteen of his wives in the Lion House, as Brigham tended to do whenever time permitted. His children, also, for the most part turned out well, except that his three sons by Mary Ann did not live up to his expectations for them; not one of them, despite ordinations by their father, assumed a leading role in the church hierarchy once their father died.

But the very number of his wives led to lampooning by immortal humorist Mark Twain and others. The late professor Stanley Hirshson in his biography, *The Lion of the Lord*, tells of an occasion in the 1860s in Salt Lake City when a woman came to Brigham seeking advice. After he had given it, he wished to record the exchange in his notes. He said: "Let me see, sister, I forget your name." Shocked, the woman snapped, "My name? Why I am your wife." Young asked when they had been married. She told him. He consulted an account book, slapped his knee, and said: "Well, I believe you are right. I knew your face was familiar."

This kind of anecdote was inevitable when you consider that during his lifetime Brigham Young married fifty-five wives and fathered fifty-eight children. Despite the church's theological justification—articulated by Brigham Young—that such wholesale procreation produced worldly bodies for free-floating spirits who, once born and baptized, could increase the population of Mormons and then, when grown, help build their desert Zion, their kingdom of God, such behavior is clearly excessive. It could also be outright abusive. Sealings were often requested for plural wives only just attaining their teen years; in many such instances, these very young women were as many as fifty years younger than their intended celestial husbands. Such arrangements are not made among equals, among consenting adults. There are even known cases of requests for sealings to females not yet in their teens.

Despite the passage of the Morrill Act outlawing polygamy in 1862, the Mormons continued the practice as official church doctrine for twenty-eight more years. When Congress strengthened the Morrill Act with the Edmunds Act, the Mormons continued to go their own way and flout federal law and federal authority, a legacy Brigham Young vigorously advocated for, though largely behind the scenes after his removal as territorial governor in 1858.

In the 1870s, in Brigham Young's last years, he was deeply embarrassed by the divorce case brought against him by his estranged former plural wife, Ann Eliza Young, who published a best-selling book exposing Brigham in particular and Mormon polygamy in general. The negative publicity from this messy and very public divorce combined with the equally negative publicity surrounding the ongoing outrage over the Mountain Meadows Massacre kept anti-Mormon sentiment running high among non-Mormon Americans in the years after the Civil War. While the Civil War raged and during the hectic and contentious years of Reconstruction, the Mormon issue had occupied a back burner in Washington. But by the 1870s, the Mormon issue was once again front and center, and the two main points of contention were the practice of polygamy and the investigation of the Mountain Meadows Massacre.

There can be no doubt that negative publicity on these two points retarded Utah from attaining statehood for over four decades. Of the two main reasons for the continued rejection of Utah's bid for statehood, beyond question polygamy was the weightier impediment. The Mountain Meadows Massacre had achieved a partial—though unjust— resolution when scapegoat John D. Lee suffered execution by firing squad in 1877 while his accomplices went free; but polygamy lingered as a festering sore for another thirteen years. Only when church president Wilford Woodruff officially repealed the doctrine of polygamy in 1890 did Utah receive serious consideration for statehood, and even then it took another half dozen years before Utah became the forty-fifth state on January 4, 1896. When Utah attained statehood and came fully under federal governance, any chance for Brigham Young's dream of a totally independent theocracy evaporated forever.

CHAPTER 27

LEGACY

— • —

Curiosity about Brigham Young in particular and about Mormons in general spread worldwide after the Utah War ended in 1858. Horace Greeley, the most famous American newspaperman of the nineteenth century, came west to interview Brigham in 1859. The Mormons made good copy, and people everywhere wanted to know more about what Brigham Young was like. Of course, a large part of this curiosity was prurient. The practice of polygamy titillated the popular imagination. Proving beyond doubt his high intelligence and his prudence—when not in the grips of residual anger over mistreatment of Mormons—Brigham would not allow himself to be drawn into free-ranging interviews with outsiders, and he was especially careful over the last nineteen years of his life. To Greeley he stated his positions flatly; he would not countenance invasions of his privacy where his multiple wives and many children were concerned.

A year later, Englishman Richard F. Burton, the Victorian explorer, intellectual, and linguist extraordinaire, spent a year traveling around the Utah Territory. Though no one thought to call it that back then, Burton was an early anthropologist with a strong interest in rituals and social customs, especially as they were related to sexual mores within a community. Greatly intrigued by the Mormon practice of polygamy, Burton sought to query Brigham in great and minute detail about his sexual relations with his plural wives. The inquisitive Englishman got virtually nowhere. Brigham adamantly refused to answer questions he considered inappropriate and invasive. Of course touring the Beehive House and the Lion House fascinated Burton, but Brigham refused him intimate domestic details about how he related to his wives and children within them.

The following year, 1861, Mark Twain showed up while traveling west with his older brother Orion, who had been appointed the first secretary of the Nevada Territory. While passing through the Utah Territory, the brothers stopped at Salt Lake City for two days. Back then, Twain, only twenty-six years old and not yet famous, still used his real name, Samuel Clemens. On this western junket he was gathering material for his book, *Roughing It*, and he played the visit with Brigham as an occasion for broad humor built around the domestic problems of having so many wives and so many children. Twain indulged in wholesale japery about which number a wife would have and how a polygamous husband would unavoidably forget the names of so many children. Facetiously, Twain described Brigham as having ordered a bed constructed for his wives seven feet long but with a headboard ninety-six feet wide. The image of the widows sitting up in the widest bed ever built became a famous newspaper caricature when Brigham died sixteen years later. Twain, over the top as usual, described the wives as snoring in unison and so loudly that they sucked in the walls of the house like a bellows, preventing Brigham from getting any sleep. In fact, Brigham slept alone.

The famous newspaper caricature of Brigham's wives, printed after his death. *Library of Congress*

As much fodder as polygamy supplied for broad humor and salacious comment, it was, as we've seen, beyond doubt the major factor preventing Utah's attainment of statehood. More than any other aspect of Mormonism, polygamy galvanized and crystallized vilification of America's one homegrown religion and hardened resistance to its broad acceptance, and that of its followers. Outsiders viewed polygamy with repugnance, and Republicans, as mentioned, lumped it with slavery as another abominable form of human exploitation and abuse, in this instance of women and children only. From a modern perspective, knowing what we do of human rights and psychology, it's hard to gainsay the nineteenth-century Republican position that the practice of polygamy was "barbaric," to use the word often applied in the popular press.

But Brigham was not deterred. As president of the church, he continued to pursue all the policies he had put in place decades ago. The missionary work flourished, and new communities of Mormons proliferated in the Utah Territory and in the West in general, especially in

the neighboring states. His dream of Mormon economic self-sufficiency
was fulfilled. Mormon industry and business acumen are legendary to
this day. Brigham's promotion of education continued apace, and, in
fact, the British explorer and anthropologist Richard F. Burton took
special note of Brigham's school for his own children and of his focus
on the importance of education for all Mormons. Both the University
of Utah and Brigham Young University benefited when Brigham sent
an entourage of Mormon educators on an inspection tour and fact-
finding mission throughout Europe. This group visited many of Europe's
great universities and returned with knowledge and insights quickly
applied to both universities founded by Brigham.

Brigham continued to tour the Mormon communities throughout
the Utah Territory and in the adjacent states. He also took a personal
interest in the construction of spectacularly beautiful temples in all of
them. His interest in these construction projects was all-encompassing,
just as it had been in the cases of the temples in Kirtland and in Nauvoo, in Salt Lake City and in St. George, the spa-like town in southern
Utah Territory. The old master carpenter and builder in Brigham
wanted to oversee every detail of construction and of interior decoration in many of these temples in satellite communities. Regrettably, he
did not live to see the completion of the imposing Mormon Tabernacle in Salt Lake City.

It was not until nearly two decades after Brigham's death, and half a
dozen years after the Mormons officially abandoned polygamy under
the leadership of Wilford Woodruff in 1890, that Utah became the forty-
fifth state admitted to the Union—on condition that the state legislature
pass a law banning polygamy—on January 4, 1896. No doubt Brigham's
spirit would smile from eternity to learn that a 2012 Gallup poll rated
Utah the top state in which to live. He would smile the more broadly
remembering all the advice he had received—and ignored—to push on
to California with all its virtues as an earthly paradise.

In late February of 1873, Brigham returned from a brief respite in St. George. His guest there had been his great friend, lawyer Thomas L. Kane of Philadelphia, now a retired general. Kane had brought along his wife and his two sons. Upon Brigham's return to Salt Lake City, he suddenly announced his resignation as president of the Deseret National Bank and of Zion's Cooperative Mercantile Institution. Brigham's management of the cooperative over the years had caused hard feelings among the non-Mormon businessmen and merchants in Utah because the cooperative extended favored-nations privileges to Mormons that were denied to non-Mormons, a form of commercial discrimination.

At this time in early 1873, Brigham also relinquished a number of his prominent positions in the church hierarchy. Significantly—to give an idea how extensive Brigham's church responsibilities were—twelve men replaced him in covering all aspects of these responsibilities. Now a very rich man, having guided the community of Saints to great prosperity in everything ranging from agriculture to milling to mining to retailing to railroading to banking to construction and beyond, Brigham took more time in his retirement years to meditate and pray and to nurture his family.

Four years later, after his retirement from his public duties, on the evening of August 23, Brigham fell ill. He had a ruptured appendix. He died quietly six days later, surrounded by his family. A very short while after his son, John Willard Young, had told his dying father to receive anointment and sealing rites, Brigham said, "Amen," then paused before adding, "That's all right."

Thus ended a life worthy of considerable admiration. Like his talents and virtues, however, Brigham Young's character flaws and shortcomings were outsized. When he sensed a threat, he could become quick to seek dominance. When things went wrong, he could be quick to exonerate himself and affix blame elsewhere. When someone disagreed with him, or worse, thwarted his will, he could be bullying and dictatorial. But in

the main, he was a man of measured judgment and huge accomplishments, especially in his early heroic years as leader of the Mormons after
the murder of Joseph Smith. His leadership on the exodus west from
Illinois to Utah is exemplary.

Brigham Young had serious failings. He exhibited very questionable
judgment in following Joseph Smith's lead on polygamy—after all,
Brigham at first recoiled from it and said he had never so wanted the
comfort of the grave as when faced with its prospect. His embrace of the
doctrine of "blood atonement" justified lynchings and at least one castration. He was responsible for scattered outbreaks of violence against
the Native Americans. His faulty judgment in the handcart debacle led
to hundreds of deaths. His lapse in judgment, in combination with
President James Buchanan's gross stupidity, led to the Utah War. And
finally, his impetuosity and foolhardiness in fomenting war fever and
fear of outsiders during the Utah War led to murders, including the
atrocity of the Mountain Meadows Massacre. But despite these failures,
Brigham Young lived a life of great achievements. Charged with many
nearly superhuman responsibilities, he discharged them admirably. And
as a colonizer, he has no peer in American history.

What Brigham Young and the Mormons have accomplished in the
last one hundred and eighty-three years is impressive. Indeed, some of
their accomplishments are monumental, not least their works of Christian charity and benevolence extended to millions of disadvantaged
people worldwide. Simply to visit Salt Lake City and stand in front of
the Mormon Tabernacle is an awe-inspiring experience. That experience,
and everything else that the Latter-day Saints have accomplished, was
brought to reality largely through the drive, resourcefulness, energy,
vision, devotion, faith, grit, and genius of this one man, Brigham Young.

ACKNOWLEDGMENTS

M y agent and friend Alexander C. Hoyt deserves thanks for unstinting help and support throughout the writing of this book. Gratitude goes out as well to Alex Novak, publisher at Regnery History, and to my editor there, Elizabeth Kantor, whose intelligence, commitment, and judgment never faltered.

As some books are written behind the headlines, this book has been written behind the historians. Without the assistance of the biographers listed in the bibliography, this book would not exist. The biographies of Leonard J. Arrington and Francis M. Gibbons, both Mormon historians, give wonderful accounts of early church history and the heroic exodus to the West. They are, however, less impartial about Mormon history once the Utah settlement occurs. Stanley P. Hirshson and John G. Turner have each written excellent and indispensable secular and scholarly biographies of Brigham Young. Professor Hirshson's book is slightly dated because he did not have available to him the archival material made available more recently to Professor Turner. If you read only one book, read Professor Turner's. Thoroughly researched from material unavailable to the earlier biographers, Professor Turner's book is equitable and measured throughout, giving a fuller account of Mormon accomplishments and failures, as well as of Brigham Young's virtues and flaws. Moreover, though a book of profound scholarship, Professor Turner's biography is beautifully written, wonderfully well-paced, and compulsively readable. I relied on it throughout and it was of inestimable help to me.

Eugene E. Campbell wrote an informative introduction to *The Essential Brigham Young*, and Dean C. Jessee edited and introduced the wonderful collection titled *Letters of Brigham Young to His Sons*. Both books helped me to understand the mind, spirit, heart, soul, and character of Brigham Young.

At the Heermance Memorial Library in Coxsackie, New York, Director Linda Doubert and her staff proved indefatigable in aiding my research. I'm grateful to all of them: Lynn Erceg, Juliana Ferenczy, Lorri Field, Christine Reda, Sandy Stephen, and Jacqueline Whitbeck.

Friends Eddie Bell, Ed Carpenter, Larissa Noon Dougherty, Yvette Durant, Michael Goedhuis, Geoff Hannell, Shelly Hebert, Gene Mydlowski, Margaret S. Neilly, Ahouva Rubinstein, and Ed Scott were always good for encouragement when needed.

Many thanks to my wife, Lynn, who, as ever, was steadfast, forbearing, helpful, patient, and loving.

BIBLIOGRAPHY

Arrington, Leonard J. *Brigham Young: American Moses*. Urbana and Chicago: University of Illinois Press, 1986.

Bushman, Richard. *Joseph Smith and the Beginnings of Mormonism*. Urbana and Chicago: University of Illinois Press, 1984.

————. *Joseph Smith: Rough Stone Rolling: A Cultural Biography of Mormonism's Founder*. With the assistance of Jed Woodworth. New York: Alfred A. Knopf, 2005.

Gibbons, Francis M. *Brigham Young: Modern Moses, Prophet of God*. Salt Lake City: Deseret Book Company, 1981.

Hirshson, Stanley P. *The Lion of the Lord: A Biography of Brigham Young*. New York: Alfred A Knopf, 1969.

Smith, Joseph, Jr. *The Book of Mormon*. Salt Lake City: The Church of Jesus Christ of Latter-day Saints, 1986.

Turner, John G. *Brigham Young: Pioneer Prophet.* Cambridge, Massachu-
    setts and London, England: The Belknap Press of Harvard Univer-
    sity Press, 2012.
Young, Brigham. *The Essential Brigham Young.* Foreword by Eugene E.
    Campbell. Salt Lake City: Signature Books, 1992.
————. *Letters of Brigham Young to His Sons.* Edited and introduced
    by Dean C. Jesse with a foreword by J. H. Adamson. Salt Lake City:
    Deseret Book Company, 1974.

INDEX

"School of the Prophets," 60–61

Sconce, John, 49–50

Scott, John, 125

Scripture, 25–26, 89, 92

"sealing," 91–92, 118, 206–7, 209, 212–13, 219

"Second Anointing," 104–5

"Second Endowment," 108–9

Second Great Awakening, 23–24

Secretary of War, 203–4

Seeley, Isaac, 91

Seeley, Lucy Ann Decker, 91

seminary, 42, 60, 88, 179

Seneca, New York, 40

separation of church and state, 99, 166, 168, 184

sextants, 137, 145–46

Sharp, Thomas, 101

Sherburne, 8–10

Shrewsbury, Massachusetts, 3–4, 10

Sierra Nevadas, 143–44, 164, 175

Smith, Don Carlos, 62–63

Smith, Don Carlos (Joseph's son), 87

Smith, Elias, 201

Smith, Emma, 35, 64, 92, 109–10, 206

Smith, George A., 78, 82, 120

Smith, Hyrum, 102–4, 113–14

Smith, John (Joseph's uncle), 40

Smith, John L. (manager of the trading post), 143

Smith, Joseph, 2, 102–4, 113–16, 166, 176

controversy of, 70–73, 88–89

finances of, 65–67

friendship with Brigham, 39, 42, 59–63, 77, 80–87, 91, 109, 121–23, 150, 161–63

leadership by, 38, 42–45, 50–51, 53, 55–56, 75

marriage of, 91–92, 205–8

politics of, 94–95, 97

as prophet, 26–30

teachings of, 178–80, 190, 220

Smith, Joseph, III, 110

Smith, Joseph, Jr., 34–35

Smith, Samuel, 25–26, 30

Smith, William, 56, 62, 65, 109–10

Smoot, Abraham O., 158–59

Snow, Erastus, 146, 163

Snow, Lorenzo, 163

Snow, Warren, 186

Soda Springs, 143

South, the, 187, 210

Southwest, the, 163

Spirit, the, 33, 55

Steuben County, 11

St. George, Utah, 180, 218–19

St. Louis, Missouri, 6, 93, 99, 118, 175, 179–80, 189

Stout, Hosea, 120, 125

Strang, James, 110–11, 213